# Making Shadow Boxes and Shrines

GLOUCESTER MASSACHUSETTS

# Making Shadow Boxes
# and Shrines

Kathy Cano-Murillo

ROCKPORT
PUBLISHERS

First published in the United States of America by
Rockport Publishers, Inc.
33 Commercial Street
Gloucester, Massachusetts 01930-5089
Telephone: (978) 282-9590
Fax: (978) 283-2742
www.rockpub.com

**Library of Congress Cataloging-in-Publication Data**
Cano-Murillo, Kathy.
  Making shadow boxes and shrines / Kathy Cano-Murillo.
        p.    cm.
  ISBN 1-56496-895-2 (paperback)
  1. Assemblage (Art) 2. Shrines. 3. Box making. 4. Souvenirs (Keepsakes)  I. Title.
TT910.C36  2002
745.593—dc21                                    2002005593

ISBN 1-56496-895-2

10 9 8 7 6 5 4 3 2 1

Design: Red Alert Design
Layout and Production: *tabula rasa* graphic design
Cover Image: Bobbie Bush Photography - www.bobbiebush.com
Interior Photography: Saunders Photography and also Bobbie Bush Photography - www.bobbiebush.com

Special thanks to the family of Joseph Cornell.

Printed in Singapore

*To my husband, Patrick, and my children, DeAngelo and Maya, for showing me the power of unconditional love and affection and for unknowingly allowing me to "borrow" some of their favorite toys for this book.*

# Contents

Introduction                                                      8
About Shadow Boxes and Shrines                                   10
The Basics of Making Shadow Boxes and Shrines                    14

PERSONAL EXPRESSION                                              20
*Shrines in Everyday Life*                                       22
Star Gazer Reflection Box                                        24
Fairy Tale Box                                                   26
Asian Princess Desk Shrine                                       28
Assemblage Trinket Box                                           30
Divine Love Box                                                  32
Italian Grotto Narrative Box                                     34

MEMORY KEEPING                                                   38
*Public Memorials*                                               40
London Calling Suitcase Shrine                                   42
Seaside Vacation Box                                             44
Newborn Baby Box                                                 46
To Life: Just the Beginning Wedding Wall Shrine                  48
Forever Friends Shadow Box                                       50
Bowen Island Box                                                 52
"My Little Muffins" Children's Toy Box                           54

TRIBUTES TO HISTORY AND CULTURE                                 56
*Joseph Cornell*                                                 58
Joseph Cornell Tribute Box                                       60
Colorful Casitas                                                 62
World Series Collectibles Box                                    64
Blue Elvis                                                       66
Tiki Tribute                                                     68
Alien Invasion!                                                  70

TRIBUTES TO HOPES AND DREAMS    72
*Hopes and Dreams*    *74*
In Loving Memory Pocket Shrines    76
Garden Angel Shrine    78
Voyage of Discovery Shrine    80
Matchbox Lapel Pins    82
A Soldier's Prayer Shrine    84
Wishful Thinking: Inspirations for the Creative Cook    88
Kwanzaa Keepsake Box    90

SHARING CELEBRATIONS    92
*El Día de los Muertos*    *94*
Desert Moon Dancer Puppet Box    96
American Pop Shrine    98
Classic Romance Shadow Box    100
Día de los Muertos Pet Altar    102
New Orleans Bingo Angel Shrine Box    104
Anniversary Box    106
Whimsical Angel Box    108

GALLERY    110
Altar to Ancestral Spirits    112
Memento Mori Altar    113
Kuan Kung Prosperity Shrine    114
The Ultimate RV Shrine    115
Sanctuary Altar    116
Le Café de los Muertos    117
Madonna Shrine    118
Weathervane Shadow Box Cabinet    119

Contributors    120
Resources    122
About the Author    125
Acknowledgments    127

# Introduction

Since I was a child, building shrines has always been a passion of mine, though in my early years, I did not quite know what a shrine was. I remember being in my bedroom with a mouthful of thumbtacks, as I stood tippytoed on my new, hot-pink shag carpet. With my arms stretched upward, I spent many nights rearranging dozens of my cherished *Teen Beat* magazine photos of David Cassidy and Donny Osmond on my wall. The photos were constantly being replaced; Cassidy and Osmond were rotated out for Johnny Rotten and the Go-Gos. Soon other objects were happily added: ticket stubs, record album covers, notes from friends, awards, dolls, bumper stickers, magazine ads, ribbons. The maniacal collection went on.

My fascination with impromptu assemblages began to overflow into other areas of my life. By way of pins, glue, nails, and tape, my notebooks, locker, car, desk, and even clothes were all covered with offbeat trinkets that inspired me and made me happy—so happy that I wanted to share them with the world.

Fast-forward to present day. I was at home the day I received the call to author this book. I gasped with delight, but hesitation soon followed. Could I live up to the extraordinary theme? What do I know about shrines? But as I held the receiver in my hand, my eyes wandered and I looked at my surroundings. There was my obsessively decorated bulletin board filled with sentimental reminders, a gourmet espresso shrine in the kitchen that housed four machines, the arrangement of framed family pictures and keepsakes on my fireplace, the outdoor patio that housed my Virgin of Guadalupe statue surrounded by colorful flowers and candles. Not to mention my computer monitor was covered with stickers, news headlines, and jewelry. I was a living ode to shrines. I enthusiastically accepted the offer with 100 percent confidence and excitement.

During the early stages of coordinating *Making Shadow Boxes and Shrines*, the tragic events of September 11, 2001, took place. My first visit to Manhattan had only been two months earlier, and I had fallen madly in love with the city. Within a few days, I took in Broadway plays, shopping in Greenwich Village, SoHo's coffee bars, nightclubs, restaurants, poetry readings, the financial district, and more. I squeezed nearly every sightseeing opportunity into my makeshift itinerary.

I was driving to work when I heard the live coverage of the collapse of the south tower. I closed my tear-filled eyes and said a prayer as I listened to the unbelievable, horrific news as it unfolded. At that moment, creating special tributes to the things and people we love—and sometimes have lost—became so much more meaningful, not only to me but also to everyone who lived through the traumatic experience. I vowed that each page of this book would be a reflection of all the happiness and joy that life has to offer.

I hope you notice.

My husband, Patrick, and I created this piece on the night of September 11, 2001, in honor of the Twin Towers and the lives that were tragically lost that morning. It still hangs in our art studio, and we plan to keep it there always.

# About Shadow Boxes and Shrines

People, places, and passions. These categories—and everything in between—mold the peculiar preferences that make up our individual personalities. Without them we would all be identical, dull, dronelike beings. Imagine how much fun that would be at a cocktail party. But because of one person's penchant for extreme sports and another's contentment with needlepoint, the world is a remarkable place filled with an abundance of interesting people to meet. Yet there is one common thread that ties us all together: the need for self-expression.

Enter *Making Shadow Boxes and Shrines.* This book is all about and for you. Its only purpose is to help you identify and celebrate the details that make you stand apart from everyone else in the universe. Assembling a signature shrine or shadow box is a wonderful method in which to do so. Not to mention, there's a chance to learn something new about what makes you tick.

## Shadow Boxes: Anything but Wall Flowers

Shadow boxes have recently come into their own singular style. They are typically composed of several items that relay a story or message. The most familiar of these are found in churches, where a series of them line the walls, and each shows a station of the cross. As an art form, they are now commonly created thanks to the visionary works of artists such as Joseph Cornell (see pages 60 – 61) and as an expanded, contemporary method of memory keeping.

The concept is as meaningful as it is appealing: a box or other type of container is used to house an arrangement of pictures, mementos, and other dimensional objects that relate to the topic of choice. The items are then secured in place in a balanced fashion so that the box can be hung on a wall or set atop a table. Shadow boxes are also a classy way to preserve special items such as tickets, diplomas, brochures, or autographs. These eventually become personalized time capsules.

## Shrines: An Ancient Art

The concept of gathering special objects and assembling them into a thought-provoking form, such as a shrine, is nothing new. Throughout the centuries, in all corners of the planet, this has been done. In Greece, there were the great Parthenon Marbles that housed a glorious, 40-foot-tall statue of the goddess Athena, lined with shimmering gold and pure ivory. In France, Notre Dame is not just a tribute to religion but also to the masons who chiseled by hand every gargoyle and detailed groove. Other powerful sites include gigantic golden Buddha statues in the East, the towering spires of the Islamic mosques that call for prayer, the haunting grounds of England's Stonehenge, the Indian palace of the Taj Mahal, which was built by an emperor in memory of his favorite wife, as well as the breathtaking Egyptian and Aztec pyramids.

The United States has its own collection of shrinelike masterpieces, such as the sacred burial grounds of Native Americans, the Vietnam Veterans memorial, Mount Rushmore, and the regal Lincoln Memorial, not to mention the natural wonders of Mother Nature created without the help of humanity.

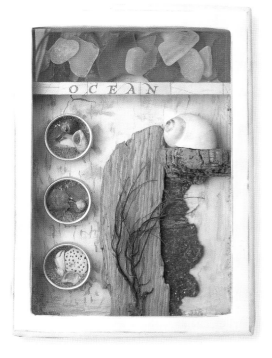

## Your Modern-Day Shadow Box or Shrine

Don't let these overwhelming examples intimidate you. And if this is unfamiliar territory, relax. Creating a personal shadow box or shrine doesn't have to be an exhaustive or life-altering undertaking. Nor does your shadow box or shrine have to be elaborate or carry a heavy message. All you need is a willing imagination, a dash of patience, and excitement for the subject. Dedicated time and a few basic craft materials also help. In exchange for the investment, you will ultimately have a timeless reminder of your finest personality traits as well as a fabulous art piece that captures the essence of all the people, places, and passions that have inspired your spirit.

## The Intuitive Shrine

Historical figures, exotic locations, bygone eras—everyone has something they hold in admiration, and each of us has unique ways of expressing that. Every type of individual, whether timid or boisterous, has built a shrine or shadow box or two in their lifetime, without even realizing it. It's natural for us to find a visual way to focus on our inner strength, or to pay respect to ancestors, or even just to have serendipitous assemblage close by that will inspire a happy grin. The approaches are endless. Think of the single photo on a windowsill or a computer monitor layered with desk toys and stickers.

## A Sacred Place

Two of the most basic, universal elements of shrines are that they are usually elevated and positioned in an important spot and that the items encompassing it have a specific purpose. Examples can be seen in everything from a small roadside shrine, to an elegant mausoleum, to a dainty corner in your grandmother's room. Some people might dedicate a harmonious corner of their garden for solace, peace, and meditation. Then there are the practitioners of *feng shui*, the Chinese art of placement, who strategically place protection, money, or happiness altars to bring good fortune or to ward off negative energy. These distinctive dots serve as glimmers of our lives and those things we deem significant during our time on Earth.

The most widespread form of shrines comes by way of family history collections. Walk into almost any household and you'll likely discover a fireplace mantel, wall, tabletop, or bookcase lined with family photos. Not only is it a way to bring the past into the present, but also it can also be a method of comfort in the grieving process, perhaps by lighting a candle and saying a prayer over a loved one's image. Tangible tributes to loved ones can also found in unconventional arrangements, such as public memorials for victims of illnesses or tragic accidents.

It used to be that if you mentioned you were building an altar, people would immediately think of stereotypical Hollywood movies. On the big screen, shrinekeepers are usually disturbed stalkers or religious fanatics. Then there's always the stereotypical homely teenage girl who is obsessed with the school jock. Erase that thought. It's so far from the truth.

## It's Your Story

Shadow boxes and shrines can be silly, serious or serene. Consider *Making Shadow Boxes and Shrines* a launching pad for converting your loves and beliefs into a poignant piece of art that not only prompts curiosity but also shares a story.

Need encouragement? Look no further than the pages before you. The following chapters contain imaginative examples that range in a variety of mediums including woodworking, embroidery, assemblage, decoupage, collages, and more. But you don't need an advanced level of skill to assemble an alluring altar or whimsical wall box. The diversity of the collection is proof of that. All types of humble hands created the pieces in this book including professional artists, proud moms, scrapbook hobbyists, crazed collectors, and more.

# The Basics of Making Shadow Boxes and Shrines

Assembling a piece of art created from treasured keepsakes and photos certainly sounds intimidating. But once you break the process down piece by piece, any feelings of anxiety morph into those of excitement as you discover a whole a new challenging side to your creativity.

The most important element is to decide upon a theme. Think of a subject that you're familiar and comfortable with. Often, all it takes is coming across a photo or memento that can be used as a centerpiece. Let the item speak to you as you develop a tone, dimension, and texture that will complement it.

Next, research. Gather as many related objects as possible that reflect your feelings. Think of this stage as "hands-on brainstorming." Go with your first instinct when collecting, and don't pass judgment. Later you will be able to sort out your collected goods according to how they fit and/or relate to your project.

Once you have accumulated the goods, move on to identifying the method by which you wish to display them. Will they fit better as a standing shrine or within a framed box? Many times a unique container on its own will launch a stream of ideas, such as the muffin pan on page 54 or the cigar box in the project on page 45. At this point, decide what type of emotion you want your project to relay. The colors and contents will play a big role.

Here are some possibilities to consider:

**For happy, whimsical, and celebratory projects,** use bright colors, glitter, toys, trinkets, rhinestones, and shells.

**For an elegant, serious, or historical look,** include earthy or muted colors, metallic highlights, foliage, lace, velvet and vintage collectibles.

**For artsy, eclectic, and thought-provoking themes,** try all types of colors, intriguing found objects, fringe, word clippings, and beads.

Of course all of these can be interchanged or substituted. The only rule is to exercise your eye for design by arranging and rearranging a layout until you find an appealing balance and structure. As far as gluing the objects in place, there are several factors to consider. If your piece is a permanent one, use an industrial strength adhesive. Some pieces, like the *Día de los Muertos* altars on page 94 are meant to go up once a year. In this case, you will not want to glue any objects so that your theme can change from year to year. If using a shadow box, decide if you want it to be under glass or exposed to allow for interactive admiration. Don't forget to assemble a proper hanging attachment depending on how heavy the box is. If using candles or incense, make sure they are located in a safe and clear area before lighting, otherwise use them for decorative purposes only.

## Preparations

- Clear a workspace large enough to allow for creativity and organized assembly.

- Line your table with inexpensive plastic or cloth to protect it from stains.

- Use clear, plastic reclosable bags to store small items.

- Keep a bottle of window cleaner, a damp sponge, and paper towels nearby to remove stubborn labels, spills, or dust.

- Tunes! Your project will be an in-depth endeavor. Pass the time by listening to your favorite music while you work. It's also fun to choose music that relates to your project. You'd be surprised how much this helps.

- Gloves, a mask, and goggles are necessary if you are building your own box or using varnish.

- Always keep a jar of clear water close by for repeated cleansing of brushes.

- Rest your hot-glue gun in a ceramic dish to avoid it dripping on your work surface and to prevent accidental burns.

# Basic craft supplies

These are your must-have materials. Many of the projects within the chapters use a spectrum of common instruments that can be found at most craft, fabric, or home-improvement stores, including the following:

**Scissors**—Yes, a standard pair is mandatory, but extra decorative pairs are even better. Use them to add a dimensional accent to paper backgrounds or fabrics. Mini scissors are useful for those hard-to-reach places.

**Adhesives**—You'll need several for each project. Elmer's glue and glue sticks are perfect for paper. A standard hot-glue gun works on most items such as wood, plastic, and cardboard. A tube of industrial-strength glue such as Goop or industrial-strength craft glue is absolutely necessary for porous, metal, and heavy items.

### Tips for gluing:

- If you have a heavy item that you need to set fast, apply a dollop of the industrial-strength craft glue to the center, and surround the edges with the hot-glue gun. This will hold the heavy item in place while the stronger glue cures.

- Use glitter glue sticks to add sparkle to edges.

- Do not use a hot-glue gun on the back of old photos or ticket stubs, as it will create black burn marks.

- To varnish photos, magazine clippings, or color copies, first brush a layer of white craft glue over the image, let dry, and then varnish.

**Tapes**—Scotch, double-sided, and carpenter's tape will come in handy.

**Ruler**—Borrow the tape measure from the garage.

**Small hammer and nails**—Useful for adding hanging attachments to the back of shadow boxes.

**Craft knives**—A set of three sizes will come in handy.

**Paints**—Satin finish spray paints are perfect for base coating. Make sure to use these in a well-ventilated area, and always wear a mask. Water-based acrylics work wonders for adding accents. Not only do they make for easy clean up but they also are nontoxic and odorless.

**Brushes**—Purchase a variety of sizes (large for base coats, thin for detail, medium for everything in between). Natural bristles are best and are useful for a variety of surfaces. Sponge applicators are fine as a substitute, although they don't offer as much control. A stencil brush is necessary if you use stencils.

**Varnish**—Several are good for a variety of uses. Sprays are excellent for even coverage. High gloss will add a brilliant shine, whereas satin will only act as a sealant. Invest in a bottle of water-based polyurethane to keep on your work area. This can easily be applied with a brush for smaller objects.

**Pencils and pens**—Pencils are perfect for marking points on surfaces. Gold, silver, and other colors of paint pens are great for adding quick embellishments.

# Basic decorative supplies

Once you have the basics, you'll want to add layers of dimensional designs that will give your project flair and personal style. While many of these items can be found at most retail stores, some will require a bit of treasure hunting. Visit local flea markets, thrift stores, import markets, or online auctions to find unique objects.

**Papers**—Invest in a variety of textures, such as tissue, napkins, patterned gift-wrap, colored card stock, handmade papers, vellum, cardboard, foam board, and any others you want to add. If you will be transferring a design, pick up a package of carbon or transfer paper. Medium-grade sand-paper will suffice to add an aged look to the edges of a shadow box.

**Odds and ends**—Fishing line for hanging items, jump rings, head pins, a roll of 36-gauge wire for holding objects in place, needlenose pliers, and tweezers for applying pressure to small items.

**Fabrics, stamps, and stencils**—Visit the local craft or fabric store to purchase material scraps such as patterned cottons, vinyl, felt, leather, fringe, appliqués, satin cording, lace, and trims. Rubber stamps and stencils are always easy to find and add a nice personal touch.

**Filler items or found objects**—These are the fun materials that will add life to your work. The following is just a portion from an endless list of options: rhinestones, fresh or plastic flowers, pliable tin, toys, coins, seashells, dry foods, buttons, jewelry, stamps, stickers, colored sand, trinkets, crystals, mosaic tile pieces, glass, mirrors, wood cutouts, marbles, rocks, strings of Mardi Gras beads, and colored raffia. Specialty items and miniatures can be found at novelty card shops, antiques stores, craft fairs, online auctions, or swap meets.

**Dimensional displays**—Look for small boxes, wood chunks, makeshift pedestals, vases, candle holders, or doll furniture that can be used within your shrine or shadow box to give objects a lift.

# The basics of making shadow boxes

The fun of making one of these projects is finding the perfect box in which to house your items. In many cases, a shallow drawer, fruit crate, suitcase, lid, or tin pan will launch a multitude of themed ideas. Consider attaching an ornate frame to your found box if it suits the project. If you cannot find a box that suits your ideals, it can be just as fun to create your own from scratch. To build a homemade shadow box, there are guidelines to follow. Here are some general notes on constructing a box, but for more detailed instructions visit your local library or bookstore for specific woodworking methods. The following are instructions for making a basic 10" X 10" (25 cm X 25 cm) shadow box that is 4" (10 cm) deep. Keep in mind measurements and thickness of wood will vary depending on your preference.

## Materials
2" X 4" (5 cm X 10 cm) pine or basswood board
10" X 10" (25 cm X 25 cm) piece of plywood, measuring ⅛" thick

## Basic Tools for Making Shadow Boxes
Jigsaw
Power miter saw, a table saw, or miter box
Table clamps
Frame clamps
Wood glue
Safety goggles
Cloth
Nails

## To Assemble
1) Wear protective goggles or earplugs for safety reasons. Cut the 2" X 4" (5 cm X 10 cm) board into four boards each measuring 10" (25 cm) long. Adjust the miter saw or fence of the table saw to a 45-degree angle, clamp one of the boards in place, and miter one end of the board a 45-degree angle. Remove the board from the table clamp, rotate, and clamp back in place in order to make another miter cut opposite from the first cut. The angles at each end should be opposing, like the pieces of a picture frame would be cut. Repeat the process on remaining three pieces of wood.

2) Apply wood glue evenly and generously to all the angled cuts on each board end. Wipe away any excess with a cloth. Use the frame clamps to hold all the edges of the box frame tightly in place. Let the glue dry for a full 24 hours before removing the frame clamps.

3) Lay the assembled wood frame flat on a table or smooth surface. Position the plywood on top of it. Attach with nails for maximum hold. If making a more delicate box, wood glue or hot-glue will also work.

4) Sand or prime as desired.

## Variation
For easier assembly without mitering, attach wood pieces with corrugated nails.

# CHAPTER 1

# Personal Expression

The beauty of personal expression is that there are no rights or wrongs. A refrigerator might be covered with a messy multitude of magnets, clippings, and photos or with a symmetrical arrangement of classy framed photos. Each approach makes a profound statement about the person behind the creation. Even if you have a bare refrigerator door and only one framed picture, that doesn't mean you have nothing to offer. This chapter will help you to pinpoint your favorite places, foods, things, people, and hobbies and to creatively present them in a fetching assemblage that is your own signature style.

Before tackling a project, record your thoughts, inspirations, and memories. Grab a pen and paper and find a relaxing spot to brainstorm. Think of Julie Andrews belting out a chorus of "My Favorite Things." That's the kind of list you want, because personal expression is all about the combination of styles that are you—and only you—know what those are. Here are a few questions to get you started:

What colors represent my personality? What are my guilty pleasures (things I'm embarrassed to admit I love)? What makes me the happiest? What is something I'm most proud to have done or made? When is the last time I did something really funny?

The answers will be the foundation of your art piece. Use materials from magazines, second-hand shops, and relatives to find items related to your list. Visit the craft store for supplies and accessories to embellish your project. Most importantly, break out that coveted box of mementos from the closet. These will become the centerpiece of a shrine or shadow box that's truly unique to you.

By recycling an old wooden Coca-Cola case, Ralph "Mr. Shrine" Wilson created a heavenly shadow box to honor his favorite religious figures. He used marbles, bottle caps, Popsicle sticks, and glitter to embellish his whimsical creation.

Ralph Wilson

# Shrines in Everyday Life
## by Michelle Craig

Connecting with objects that inspire and motivate us as individuals is the art of creating personal shrines, altars, and places. It's a concept that has become increasingly popular as people are finding self-empowerment through personal expression.

"We have a hole in a sense of who we are that needs to be filled," says artist and college instructor Kay Grosso. "When our spirits are tired, flat, and dry … that's where that dark hole is. What we want is to put the light in there."

It is common to enter a home to find a bookcase covered in pictures of family and loved ones or to spot a piano ledge displaying treasured mementos. They provide solace in times of need and pride during times of joy. They celebrate who we are. For Grosso, creating these intimate spots and inspiring others to do the same is an important aspect of her life, personally and professionally. She is the originator of a motivational program that utilizes storytelling, film, and cultural exchanges to encourage women to grow spiritually. One activity invites the women to transform ordinary cigar boxes into self-reflective altar boxes.

In her program, Grosso offers fabrics, stones, shells, ribbon, lace, and more. She suggests that the women select the items that speak to them, followed by adding personalized photos and trinkets. She says these cigar box altars are popular with young girls who look to them as an interactive hope chest or diary.

There are always those who don't need coaching on how to indulge in personal expression. Anyone who enters Frances Fitzhugh's home in Glendale, Arizona, is quickly drawn to several expressive places that feature her love for bells, angels, and family. One of her most beloved areas is the fireplace mantel, which displays special, personal items such as a musical gourd instrument, a book about Native Americans, hand-carved African spoons, and an artistically handmade Native American turtle. Together these items visually relay a side of her life that she deems sacred. The mantel serves as the room's focal point, not only because of its structure but also because it hosts a celebration of her African and Native American culture.

"It sets a tone for the home," Fitzhugh explains. "It's an expression of myself, an inner expression manifested outside."

All different forms of personal expression—art, music, writing, or creating shrines and altars—are about rejoicing for our soul and our self. Often we are consumed with taking care of and empowering others. But taking time for our own personal expression allows us to remember, honor, hope, and dream.

# Star Gazer Reflection Box

When you peek into this glittery-mirrored box, you can't help but smile because these shiny mirrors are meant to embrace and inspire self-reflection, no matter what your present mood might be. Add a dash of personal style by using specific objects that are meaningful to you. In any case, twinkling golden stars floating within a midnight blue background will always do the trick.

### Materials

Sequins or rhinestones

Shooting star ornament

Star-shaped cutouts

Mirror, 4" × 4" (10 cm × 10 cm)

Bag of mini mirrors

12" × 12" (30 cm × 30 cm) plywood panel, about ¼" thick (5 mm)

Two 2" × 4" × 12" (5 cm × 10 cm × 30 cm) wood boards

Two 2" × 4" × 9" (5 cm × 10 cm × 23 cm) wood boards

Acrylic paints, 3 or 4 colors of choice

Acrylic paintbrushes

Glitter glue

Long nails

Glue gun

Hammer

Basic craft supplies (see page 17)

1) Nail the 2" × 4" (5 cm × 10 cm) boards to the hardwood panel to form a square shadow box 3" in depth.

2) Paint the box in colors of choice.

3) Using industrial-strength craft glue, attach the large mirror to the center of the box's interior and the small mirrors around the frame.

4) Hammer three nails into each inner side of the box. Attach a star on top of each nail with the glue gun. Apply a layer of industrial-strength craft glue underneath each star to securely hold it in place.

5) Decorate the remainder of the box, stars, and mirrors with glitter, rhinestones, and paint. Add the shooting star ornament to the upper-right corner.

### TIPS

- Nails and extra stars may also be added around the outside of the box for an added dimensional effect. Use smaller nails if you are creating a smaller box.
- Not into stars? Other themes will work just as well—snowflakes, chile peppers, coins, vintage jewelry, or buttons.

**Dimensions** 12" X 12" X 4" (30 cm X 30 cm X 10 cm)          **Artist** Audrey Anna Diaz

# **Fairy Tale** Box

To escape a busy lifestyle venture into the magical world of fairy tales. This wall box captures that storybook essence. Concealed in this "forest" is a golden key to a wondrous palace. Old bark, lichen, and other natural objects were combined to create a dark, mysterious setting to contrast with the gold. This castle was inspired by medieval illuminated manuscripts.

**Materials**

Cigar box

Basswood strips, 1" (3 cm) wide

Card stock (for the castle)

Imitation gold leaf & size

Glass

Balsa wood strips, ⅛" (3 mm)

Copper foil tape

Bronze and copper patina sets

Found objects: bark, moss, lichen, butterfly wing, tiny wasp's nest, chestnut casing (used for the key)

Leaf skeletons

Small key

Cutting mat

Sandpaper

Craft brushes

Acrylic gel medium

Gesso

Brown acrylic paint

Walnut-tone wood stain

Glass cutter

Ruler

Basic craft supplies (see page 17)

Basic tools for making shadow boxes (see page 19)

1) Mark a ¼" (2 cm) border around the edge of a cigar box lid. Wear safety goggles and clamp the box securely to your work surface. Cut a hole in the lid with a jigsaw, following the drawn lines and using an edge guide.

2) Sand the edges and the outside of the box smooth to remove varnish or lettering. Wipe clean with a damp cloth. Stain the box and attach a hanging device on back.

3) Create a façade with basswood: Measure the opening on the box and mark the inside measurements on the wood. Cut wood using a miter box and a saw. Glue the frame together, let the glue set, and paint with gesso. Let dry, and coat the frame with bronze patina. Paint the copper patina inside the upper half of the box to create the sky behind the castle).

4) Draw a small castle on card stock, measuring approximately 3" × 3" (8 cm × 8 cm). Cut out the castle with the craft knife. Coat with the gold-leaf size and imitation gold leaf. Gently burnish the leaf and antique it with a glaze of gel medium and burnt umber acrylic paint. Repeat last step with the key.

5) Cut two 4" × 4" (10 cm × 10 cm) pieces of glass, guiding glasscutter with a ruler. Sandwich the castle between the two pieces of glass and seal the edges with copper foil tape. Paint craft glue around the back edge of the glass and mount it on ⅛" (3 mm) balsa strips. Paint craft glue onto the back of the balsa strips and place the castle on top of the copper patina inside the box. Press down gently until glue has set.

6) Arrange bark and other natural objects inside the box, attaching them with a hot-glue gun. Secure the key inside the casing with epoxy glue. To screen the castle and key, add leaf skeletons with a dot of craft glue at top and bottom edges of leaves.

**VARIATIONS**
- Use a tinted photocopy of an old engraving for the palace.
- Photocopy images of animals from copyright-free sources, tint them with watercolors, and mount on card stock to add another element to the story.
- Use a picture frame molding instead of the bronze basswood frame.

# **Asian Princess** Desk Shrine

Despite cartoons that depict office life as a dronelike world of identical cubicles, there really are creative and subtle ways to incorporate personal expression into a workspace. Assembling one of these small shrines is one of them. Although every job requires detailed attention to mundane duties, there's always room for a bit of innocuous, individual flair. This shrine is compact enough to set atop a computer monitor, bookshelf, or desk, yet still has enough room to carry a theme of culture, passion, or admiration. This project was created as a tribute to Asian culture. You can use it as an inspiring way to honor your own culture in everyday life away from your private home.

**Materials**

1 hinged wood triptych, 8" (20 cm) tall

1 wood base, 6" × 3" (15 cm × 8 cm)

1 standing Asian doll

Asian-inspired wrapping paper

1 small Botan rice candy box

Feng shui good luck fish

Bamboo candle

Chinese pin cushion

Asian coins

Red wood beads with Chinese lettering

Translucent paints in red, yellow, and green

Basic craft supplies (see page 17)

1) Paint the wood base and front panels of triptych using red, green, and yellow paints. Using the white craft glue, line the front center panel and the back sides of all three panels with the wrapping paper. Trim excess edges of paper.

2) With the glue gun, attach the standing triptych to the wood base, keeping the side panels open. Adhere the doll to the center of the base with industrial-strength glue and hold it place until the glue sets.

3) Glue the box of candy on the left panel and the fish on the other. Attach the pincushion and candle on either side of the doll.

4) Add the coins in a random fashion to the front and back of the shrine. Repeat the process for the beads.

**TIP**
Before gluing, arrange the items until you find a balanced design. Use industrial-strength glue for heavier items.

**VARIATION**
Be multicultural. This desk shrine can be adapted to fit any heritage. Visit local import stores to find international objects. It also works well with movie or music stars. Cover the base with magnetic paint (see Fridge Door in Resources, page 122) and then use magnetic words or pictures to make your shrine interactive.

**Dimensions** 8" X 4" (20 cm X 10 cm)                    **Artist** Kathy Cano-Murillo

# **Assemblage** Trinket Box

Once you've incorporated all your personal mementos into a fabulous work of art, it's only a matter of time before a new collection of keepsakes turns up again. While you're waiting to tackle a new masterpiece, why not create a small trinket box to hold all your tiny treasures for safekeeping? This shadow box within a box concept puts the fun in functional. Use a variety of papers and fabric to add a quaint yet classy element to the decorative contents.

**Materials**

Small recipe box with removable glass casing on lid

Small found objects with a variety of textures: figures, paint chips, recycled papers, buttons, fabric scraps, pins, or toys

Coordinating acrylic paint

Sandpaper

Basic craft supplies (see page 17)

1) Remove the glass from the box lid and set aside. Apply a base coat of paint to all areas of the box. Sand and then add another layer of paint.

2) Arrange and assemble the collage: Move the paper, fabric, and objects around to experiment with dimensional relationships and composition before applying the glue.

3) Add a light dab of industrial-strength craft glue to the box surface and begin to apply the objects one by one. If there is a heavier object, such as a toy or button, apply pressure for several minutes until it adheres properly.

4) Smooth out any air bubbles after gluing paper items. Use a cloth or cotton swab to remove excess glue.

5) As you are gluing, continue to alter the composition from your original idea—let one application inspire another. Reattach the glass to the lid and secure with glue.

**TIP**

If you are unable to locate a box with a glass lid, use a regular wood box and glue a matching-sized Plexiglas photo frame to the lid to create a covered shadow box look. Varnish the box if desired.

**Dimensions** 6" X 4" X 4" (15 cm X 10 cm X 10 cm)     **Artists** Cynthia Atkins (assemblage) and Philip Welch (woodwork)

# Divine Love Box

Divine love between man and woman is the inspiration for this richly textured framed display. The purpose is to affirm unity, balance, and respect between the masculine and feminine forces within the universe. While the Indianlike image is anchored as the focal point, the color combination of red, green, purple, and gold is just as powerful. Together these hues represent love, passion, loyalty, growth, spirituality, royalty and energy.

**Materials**

17" × 13" × 1½" (43 cm × 33 cm × 4 cm) shallow shadow box with removable frame

14" × 12" (36 cm × 30 cm) bright red mat board

10" × 8" (25 cm × 20 cm) dark red mat board

7" × 5" (18 cm × 13 cm) romantic Indian print

Assorted rhinestones in purple and blue

Assorted mosaic glass or plastic pieces in green and purple

Red beaded fringe

Gold spray paint

Hot-glue gun

1) Separate the frame from the shadow box and spray paint both gold. Let dry.

2) Enhance the print's details with paint and ink. Adhere it to the smaller mat so that it looks framed. Add rhinestones to the print for dimension. Mount the two mats to the box interior.

3) Arrange rhinestone designs on the mats to create a uniform layout. Glue the pieces in place.

4) Assemble the box and the frame.

5) Glue the colored mosaic pieces in random order around the border of the outer frame. Attach a sawtooth picture hanger to the back.

**TIP**
Look through old family photographs, postcards, magazines, wrapping paper, or copyright-free Web sites to find romantic pictures that reflect your own interpretation of divine love. For a more personal touch, create an original image on canvas board with markers, colored pencils, or acrylic paints.

**VARIATION**
Add other elements that represent balance and beauty such as crystals, power stones, or amulets.

# Italian Grotto Narrative Box

Shadow boxes can be a great way to encapsulate both the visual and emotional experiences of a memorable trip. This particular project is inspired by a visit to an Italian villa, which showcased a formal garden and a baroque grotto decorated with intricate patterns of pebble mosaics. A lingering gaze inside this box's contents conjures up thoughts of blissful strolls through overgrown gardens and curious peeks into mysterious caves.

**Materials**

Cigar box

1¼" × ⅜" (3½ cm × 1 cm) basswood strips

Photocopies of plants and insects

Two 6" × 8" (15 cm × 20 cm) fiberglass screens

Found natural objects: birch bark, moss, honeycomb, snail shells

Sand

Twigs and dried plants

Birch bark

Gesso

Acrylic paints in olive green and metallic gold

Acrylic medium

Spackle

Oil of wintergreen

Sandpaper

Hardware for hanging

Putty knife

Burnishing tool

Epoxy and craft glues

Artist brushes

Basic craft supplies (see page 17)

Basic tools for making shadow boxes (see page 19)

1) Mark out a rectangle on the lid of a cigar box so that there is a ¼" (2 cm) border around the edge. Wear safety goggles and clamp the box securely to your work surface. Cut a hole in the lid with a jigsaw following the drawn lines and using an edge guide.

2) Sand the cut edges until smooth. Sand the entire box if there is any paint or varnish on its surface. Wipe the box with a damp cloth and paint the box, inside and out, with gesso. Attach a hanging device to the back of the box.

3) Make a frame for the box front out of the basswood: Measure the box opening and mark the measurements onto the basswood (the measurements for this frame's

interior are 5" × 7" [13 cm × 18 cm]). Cut the wood using a miter box and a wood saw. Using wood glue, adhere the frame sides together and let the glue set for thirty minutes before applying the spackle with a putty knife. Smooth the spackle with a damp cloth, let it dry, then sand.

4) To transfer the plant images, tape the photocopy face down onto the frame and paint the back of the photocopy with oil of wintergreen. Burnish the image until it transfers onto the spackled surface. Stain the frame with watered-down, olive green paint, and lightly sand for an aged effect. Also coat the sides and back of the box with the same paint. Attach the frame to the front of the box with craft glue.

*(continued on page 36)*

**TIPS**
- To check if the image has been transferred to your liking, carefully lift up a corner of the photocopy as you work.
- Flatten the birch bark by soaking it in hot water and weighting it as it dries. Note: only collect birch bark from fallen branches on the ground.

## **Italian Grotto** Narrative Box—*continued*

5) Using a staple gun, attach an 8" X 6" (20 cm X 15 cm) piece of fiberglass mesh to the inside of the lid. Paint the mesh with olive green and metallic gold paints. Cut an archway out of another piece of mesh and attach it with epoxy glue to the back of the first piece at the top and bottom.

6) To create the grotto, arrange the birch bark, moss, honeycomb, and snail shells inside the box and attach with epoxy glue. Brush craft glue onto some areas and sprinkle with sand. Using a craft knife, cut a 1" (3 cm) square window in the mesh to reveal a portion of the box's interior. Attach the dried plants to the front of the mesh with epoxy glue. Highlight areas on the plants with metallic gold and copper acrylic paints.

### TIP
To further enhance the visual presence, pen a descriptive narrative to accompany it. Here's an example to get you started: *The golden bee dances on a leaf creating an intricate map. The pattern leads through the forest to the snail's grotto. The cave entrance is dark and lined with honeycomb. The passage hums with the beating of insect wings. The grotto is chalky and light; head towards the glow. Answer the riddle and the shell transforms into a perfect gem.*

### VARIATIONS
• Instead of mesh, use closely set twigs to create a forest effect in front of the grotto.
• Use plaster or a pebble mosaic instead of the birch bark to create texture inside the grotto.

**Artist** Paula Grasdal

# CHAPTER 2

# Memory Keeping

The age-old idea of delicately placing a rose within the pages of a book is as romantic as it is practical. The flower represents a moment in time, while the book preserves it. One day when that book is opened and the rose is rediscovered, it will make for an incredible story to share. This is the magic of memory keeping.

The art of assembling keepsakes into visual showpieces dates back to the seventeenth century, when creating scrapbooks emerged as a way to preserve newspaper clippings, photos, and locks of hair. Why not continue the tradition with your own time capsule?

Begin with a theme. There are many starting points: A first day at school, the big family vacation, a first car or house, a wedding, a new baby, or honoring a loved one. Then there are those offbeat occasions that are just as worthy of remembering: losing a first tooth, meeting a favorite celebrity, relaxing at the park, or braving a wild haircut.

Now it's time to get to work. Sketch out ideas that match your feelings about the memory. This will determine your colors and embellishments. If using photos, document the dates, ages, names, and locations. Separate the remaining mementos into categories according to shape, size, and texture. To add accents, visit local flea markets or thrift stores for accessories or include found objects such as postage stamps, foliage, and jewelry. Finally, record the story of the event—perhaps you can include it in the design or write it on the back of the project.

The assemblages in this chapter offer a range of colorful ideas from which to choose. Try one, or if you're daring, combine elements from several. After all, it is your memory.

The Strawberry Fields memorial to John Lennon, in New York's Central Park, is visited by hundreds of patrons each day. It's not uncommon to see flowers or mementos left at the site.

Theresa Cano

# Public Memorials

The year was 1997 when the ultimate shock of the decade ripped through the world. Diana, Princess of Wales, had passed away in a tragic car accident. Although the "commoners" like us had never met this British dignitary, we felt as if we had known her all of our lives. With the combination of her gentle demeanor, motherly grace, humanitarian deeds, and glamorous style, she fulfilled the regal criteria of what a true princess should be. It was no wonder so many individuals felt a tidal wave of grief at her unexpected passing.

But no one, not even the surviving royal family, predicted what would happen next. There at the gates of Diana's London residence of Kensington Palace, scores of admirers arrived to the grounds armed with blooming floral bouquets, oversized handmade signs, tenderly written cards, and powerful prayers. That was only the beginning. Within days, the area was further consumed with a sea of millions of sentimental offerings. It was one of the largest spontaneous shrines of its time.

Public memorials are a comforting aspect of the healing process when the life of a very special person is taken away. It's an indirect way to honor our heroes, even if we have never had the opportunity to meet them. When former Beatle John Lennon passed away in 1980, his devoted fans created the Strawberry Fields mosaic memorial in New York's Central Park. Every day of every year, hundreds of devotees visit the intricate inlay that is inscribed with the title *Imagine* to lovingly commemorate his life and body of work. The sidewalk monument became even more significant when Lennon's bandmate George Harrison lost his battle with cancer in 2001. Distraught disciples came from far and wide to pay respect while closing their tear-filled eyes and quietly humming their favorite Harrison tune.

When it comes to enshrinements for larger-than-life pop icons, the list is never ending. Marilyn Monroe, Kurt Cobain, Selena, Jim Morrison, Jimi Hendrix, Janis Joplin, and John F. Kennedy Jr. are just a handful of the ill-fated celebrities whose deaths ignited eternal flames on prayer candles. But movie and music stars aren't the only subjects of public mourning. Many times, it's the loss of ordinary people like you and me that cause the greatest pain in the hearts of others.

A magnitude of broken-hearted emotion is still being experienced to this day due to the horrendous New York City and Washington, D.C., events that took place on September 11, 2001. From fearless firefighters to professional office workers to humble cafeteria helpers—every life that was traumatized that day affected our global community. Aside from blood, clothing, and monetary donations, people of all races, ages, and cultures contributed their own visual respects. Some came by way of signs, flowers, and postcards gently laid along the edges of ground zero. Others came in the form of serenity altars in the home, adorned with flowers, photos, and letters. The Internet became a high-tech avenue for communicating voices of wisdom, sorrow, and hope. As heavy as the mood was, each sign of affection sparkled as a light of optimism. These helpless victims would forever remain in our hearts and minds.

Dotted across the country is another form of community display that is steadily growing: roadside shrines. Family and friends create these outdoor assemblages when precious lives are lost in car accidents. They are often composed of decorative plastic flowers, ribbons, poems, and a large white cross that bears the name and photo of the victim. It's a compelling symbol to passersby—many of whom offer the sign of the cross and send a blessing.

These types of shrines are especially prominent in various parts of Mexico. South of the border, the roadsides are laced with memorials, except many of these are much more elaborate than just a cross with flowers. Local artisans gracefully take this craft to new and impressive levels by incorporating advanced art techniques such as mosaics, paintings, and tinwork. They are often encased in *casitas,* or small houses, complete with festive décor, doors, glass windows, or screen panels to peek through. These Mexican tributes also are adorned with beautiful images or statues of a religious figure such as the Virgin of Guadalupe, Jesus, or a favorite saint.

Among such a diverse spectrum of public memorials, the ultimate message is clear and universal. The foundation comes with a sincere promise of everlasting remembrance and love.

# **London Calling** Suitcase Shrine

All of us have our guilty pleasures on this planet. It could be by absorbing endless hours of a travel-themed cable channel or repeated cross-Atlantic excursions to the same city. In this case, it's jolly old London, England. It's the ultimate bow of adoration for this legendary metropolis that's rich with royal history, haunting tales, and the best of pop culture. The maniacal way in which this suitcase was layered translates the extreme elation that emerged from three separate visits that spanned a period of nineteen years. For the ultimate suitcase shrine, collect as many odds and ends as you can. They will eventually add the most perfect definition to your British brouhaha. That is, except for the steamy cup of Earl Grey. That's better left in the United Kingdom.

**Materials**

Suitcase with rigid sides

London stickers, postcards, magnets, small souvenirs, personal photos

Newspaper, magazine, or tour brochure clippings

Trading cards

Small toys

Red, blue, and clear jewels

Scarf

Toy tiara

Punk Rock music buttons

English currency

Strings of beads

Magnetic poetry (London edition)

Squeeze glitter

Basic craft supplies (see page 17)

1) Thoroughly clean the surface of the suitcase with a damp cloth to remove dust or debris.

2) Sort the items by size, and choose one or two pieces that will be the focal points. Using white craft glue, first adhere all of the flat items such as postcards, clippings, and photos. Apply them in a balanced and random fashion.

3) Fill in the empty spaces with dimensional toys on the top and front of the suitcase. Use industrial-strength craft glue for heavier items. Line the borders with strings of beads.

4) There will be small, leftover spaces. Fill these in with squeeze glitter, coins, and magnetic poetry.

5) When the suitcase is completely dry, tie the scarf on the handle, and glue the tiara on the top.

**TIP**
Look for inexpensive vintage suitcases at thrift stores or yard sales. If you don't have enough souvenirs from your trips, they may be purchased through online shops or auctions. Find a sturdy stand in which to showcase your finished piece.

**VARIATION**
For a less cluttered look, use large images from an outdated London calendar as the focal point of your suitcase shrine. For a smaller piece, use a small vanity suitcase. This project can be altered to fit any vacation or favorite location.

**Dimensions** 13" X 20" (33 cm X 51 cm)          **Artist** Kathy Cano-Murillo

# **Seaside** Vacation Box

Life is a beach, and here's the proof. This box recalls a seaside vacation with shells, glass, and driftwood encapsulating a relaxing holiday. The map-covered divider creates the illusion of a water line, so the objects below appear to be in an underwater cave. The round metal containers, normally used for fishing tackle, play off the theme of the box.

**Materials**

Cigar box

Beach glass

Shells

Sand

Driftwood

Map of the ocean

Postcard fragment

Newspaper

Piece of glass to cover the box

3 containers or fishing tackle tins,
1½" (4 cm) in diameter

Rusted metal

1" × ⅜" (3 cm × 1 cm) balsa wood strips

Spackle

Spackle tape

Acrylic paint

Acrylic medium

Putty knife

Sandpaper

Two-part epoxy

Basic craft supplies (see page 17)

Basic tools for making shadow boxes
(see page 19)

1) Mark out a rectangle on the lid of a cigar box so there is a border of ¾" (2 cm) around the edge. Wear safety goggles and clamp the box securely to your work surface. Cut a hole in the lid with a jigsaw, following the drawn lines and using an edge guide.

2) Sand the rough edges of the window. Sand the box to remove paint or varnish on its surface. Wipe the box with a damp cloth and apply the spackle tape to the inside. Apply spackle with a putty knife to all surfaces of the box, then smooth the surface with a damp cloth. Let dry about one hour and then sand the spackle until smooth. Attach a hanging device to the back of the box.

3) Stain the inside of the box with watered-down acrylic paints in burnt umber, red sienna, and yellow ochre. Let dry and then lightly sand to create an aged effect. Cut two pieces of 1" (3 cm)-wide balsa to the right length for your box (this one is 6½" [17 cm]). Paint one piece white, and make a collage with fragments of torn map on the other piece, using acrylic medium. Measure ¼" (5 mm) in from the edge of the wood pieces, and with a craft knife, cut a groove in each piece for the piece of glass.

4) Glue the white piece of balsa wood with the groove facing down to the inside top of the box. Arrange the beach glass and then slide the piece of glass, measuring 6½" × 1½" (17 cm × 4 cm) into the groove. Put craft glue on the bottom and ends of the collaged piece of balsa wood and fix in place, making sure that the groove holds the piece of glass securely and the beach glass is contained.

5) Assemble the beach-combed objects inside the box and attach them with epoxy glue. Paint craft glue to the inside of the round metal containers and sprinkle with sand. Place the shells and fragments inside with some loose sand. Then glue the lids shut. For a finishing touch, paint craft glue on some areas inside the box and sprinkle with sand.

**TIP**

To create cracks in the spackle, apply thickly and dry with a hair dryer.

**VARIATIONS**
- Create small compartments inside the box with pieces of painted balsa.
- Create a mosaic of shells and pebbles inside the box.

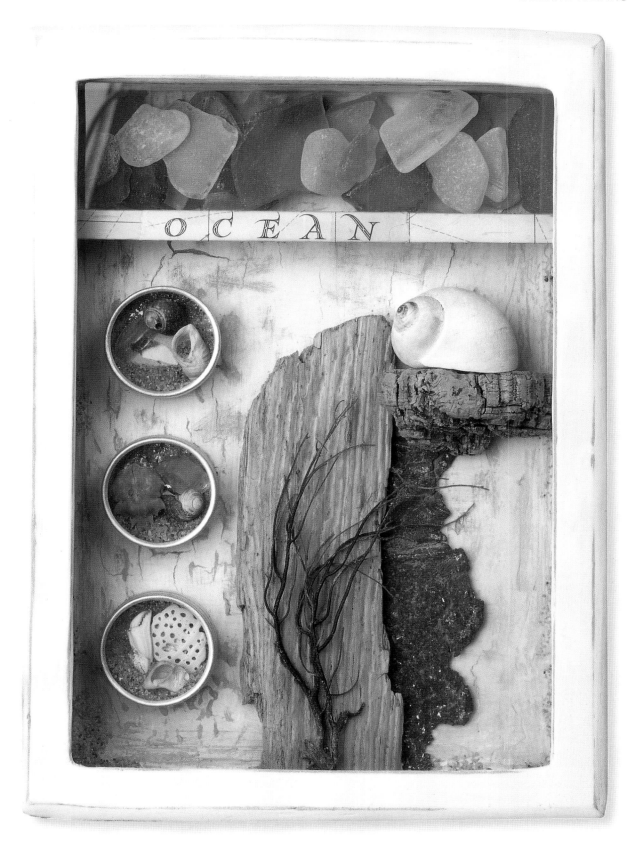

**Dimensions** 10½" X 7¼" X 1½" (27 cm X 18½ cm X 4½ cm)          **Artist** Paula Grasdal

# Newborn Baby Box

The moment the cheery stork delivers that special package to a doorstep, a baby memory book follows right behind. Packed with pages documenting all the pertinent details, the scrapbook becomes a crucial aspect to mommies and daddies who want to preserve the miracle. Somewhere in the mix of sorting the memorabilia, there are always leftover items such as wrapping paper from gifts, the baby's first diaper pin, shower party favors, and cake decorations. These tiny, underestimated odds and ends are the perfect adornments for a loving shadow box specially designed for that tiny bundle of joy.

**Materials**

8½" X 8½" X 1" (22 cm X 22 cm X 3 cm) shadow box

Miniature dollhouse dresser

Handmade papers

White, pink, yellow, and blue glue

3 miniature baby photos

2" (5 cm) baby photo

Photo ornament

Baby shower keepsakes: wrapping paper, cake decorations, diaper pins, and party favors

Cotton handkerchief

Craft foam

Ribbon

Wood banner

Acrylic paint in white

Acrylic accent paint in pink or blue

Scalloped scissors

Basic craft supplies (see page 17)

1) Apply a base coat of white acrylic paint to the entire box and the miniature dresser. Sand the edges if desired to give it an aged look. Use scalloped scissors to cut the handmade paper into strips. Use a glue stick to apply these to the border of the box's frame.

2) Adhere the wrapping paper by decoupage to the interior of the box. Take the mini dresser and stock it with some of the keepsakes. Cut the handkerchief into small squares and fold them to look like diapers. Accent the dresser with the pink or blue paint.

3) Glue the dresser in the box center and the banner at the top of the frame. Gently rip a circle from the handmade paper and attach it to the back of the 2" (5 cm) baby photo, then place it in the center of the banner.

4) Cut small images from wrapping paper and adhere them to the craft foam to create a colorful border edge. Carefully glue these along the banner and around the frame, interspersed between more small baby pictures.

5) Attach the hanging ornament with a ribbon at the bottom of the box. Add a sawtooth picture hanger for displaying.

**TIPS**
- Make color copies if you prefer not to use originals.
- Apply the photos to wood discs to create a lifted, dimensional effect.

**VARIATION**
Instead of a square shadow box, use a circular wall hanging and line with it with lace or beads.

# To Life: Just the Beginning
## Wedding Wall Shrine

In the world of weddings, vows are meant to last forever. What better way to relive the once-in-a-lifetime experience than to capture the magical memories in a stunning wall display? Much like weddings, planning is a crucial element for this project. Before the big day, recruit a loved one as the designated memory caretaker—a job that will require them to meticulously collect a variety of personal objects associated with the wedding from beginning to end. Eventually these prized possessions will be assembled into a beautiful wall shrine of eternal bliss—and a constant reminder of those special vows and that unforgettable day.

**Materials**

Shadow box with 4 shelves or compartments (door is optional)

Bridal shower, wedding, and honeymoon mementos: invitations, photos, flowers, napkins, receipts, maps, love letters, fabric swatches from clothing, table accessories, menus, sand, shells, rocks or leaves from location, and champagne corks/glasses

Basic craft supplies (see page 17)

1) Categorize the mementos into four groups: wedding, honeymoon, bride, and groom.

2) Designate a compartment in the wall shrine for each group.

3) Use a glue stick and card stock or scrapbook borders to add an elegant background to the photos or other paper objects.

4) Spend some time assembling objects in the compartments until a balanced form is achieved, then adhere to the surface. Suspend objects from the top of the compartments with string and small suction cups.

5) If your wall shrine has a door, use it to hang objects such as a garter belt, jewelry, or tie.

**TIPS**
- Decorate the outside of the wall shrine with beautiful wrapping paper from gifts or lace. To add dimension to photos, apply background layers of colored card stock.
- Use decorative scrapbook borders, die cuts, stickers, or wedding-themed accessories for added embellishments.

**Dimensions** 30" X 18" X 6" (76 cm X 46 cm X 15 cm)

**Artist** Terri O

# **Forever Friends** Photo Box

A golden moment captured on film is what this photo box is all about. Following childhood and preceding adulthood, we develop some of our most cherished relationships that will endure throughout our lives. If we do happen to lose touch with them, this project will preserve the memory just as you left it. Choose one classic image that relays the extraordinary feeling of serendipitously showing off youthful grins, gorgeous figures, and spiffy clothes. Splurge on a fancy frame, glass beads, and floral roses to enhance the beauty of your visual time capsule.

**Materials**

Old photo of a gathering of friends

6" × 8" × 1½" (15 cm × 20 cm × 4 cm) wood box

10" × 8½" (25 cm × 22 cm) wood frame

3" × 5" (8 cm × 13 cm) wood block with scalloped edge

Bag of glass seed beads

4 medium-sized fabric or dried roses

Bottle of translucent squeeze glitter

Acrylic paints in black, white, and gold

Stencil brush

Picture-hanging attachment

Basic craft supplies (see page 17)

1) Paint the box white and the frame black. When dry, stencil gold on top of both and let dry. Squeeze the translucent glitter on both surfaces and gently sweep it across with the brush to create a shimmery effect.

2) Copy an old photo in color and use a glue stick to adhere it to the wood block. Paint the ridges black and stencil with gold. Working on top of newspaper, line the top edge of the block with industrial-strength craft glue. Sprinkle the seed beads and then pat them with your finger to create an even layer. This will reduce the number of beads that will fall off. Tap the block on the paper to catch loose beads. Let it dry and then attach the block to the center of the wood box.

3) Rest the picture frame over the front of the box and line it up evenly. Hold it firmly and turn it upside down. Run a bead of hot glue along the seams where the frame and box meat to secure it and let dry.

4) Adhere a layer of seed beads around the outer edge of the frame. Glue one rose to each corner of the frame. Add a hanging attachment to the back.

**TIP**

Take extra care when lining up the frame with the box to ensure the two are sealed in a straight and even manner. Lightly tap box to remove loose seed beads. Gently remove any stragglers by hand or with tweezers.

**VARIATION**

The color scheme of this box was created for an old black-and-white photo. If using a color photo, change colors to match. Add small keepsakes around the border that are associated with the picture.

**Dimensions** 6" X 8" (15 cm X 20 cm)      **Artist** Kathy Cano-Murillo

# **Bowen Island** Box

Childhood memories from happy summer vacations ultimately contribute to our adult personalities. This project captures those significant moments to share the spirit of days gone by. This example celebrates the rocky beaches and lush forests that provided the artist endless hours of adventure on an island off the northwest coast of Canada. The homage to beloved family members comes via a baking tin and bottles that were discovered from the relative's property years later. One of these bottles contains an aged photograph of an uncle. Other found objects such as moss, feathers, and beach glass hint at a time spent outside, exploring the natural world.

## Materials

Old baking tin

Old photograph

Moss

Honeycomb

Feathers

Snail shell

Beach glass

Sand

Crab claw

Glass fragment

Photocopy of a bird

3 glass bottles

Rusted metal object

Medium-gauge wire

Awl

Basic craft supplies (see page 17)

1) Assemble photographs and natural objects in the bottles so that each container has a theme. For example, put the beach items in one bottle and the forest objects in another. Put the lids on the bottles and attach found objects on top with epoxy glue.

2) Place the tin on a scrap of plywood. Using an awl, poke two holes 1" (3 cm) apart and 2" (5 cm) below the upper-center edge of the tin. Thread a 4" (10 cm) length of wire through the holes and twist the ends together to form a loop for hanging. Arrange natural elements such as moss, bark, and honeycomb along the upper portion of the box, and glue with epoxy.

3) Age a photocopy of a bird image by tearing the edges of the paper and soaking it in strong tea. Allow the paper to dry. Using craft glue, attach the bird image to the box and let dry. Glue a fragment of glass over the bird image with craft glue (this will take several hours to set).

4) Fix the bottles inside the box with epoxy glue.

**TIP**
Look for old baking tins and bottles at antique stores or flea markets.

**VARIATIONS**
• Mount an old mirror behind the bottles to create the illusion of depth.
• To make doors cut two pieces of tin to the appropriate size, decorate with an embossing tool, and attach to the front of the box using wire as hinges.
• Instead of tin doors, cover the box front with chicken wire for a rustic look.
• Place objects in the bottles that relate to your memories of a city rather than a natural environment. Map fragments, found metal scraps, and other ephemera could replace the moss and feathers.

**Dimensions** 9" X 8½" X 2½" (23 cm X 22 cm X 5½ cm)          **Artist** Paula Grasdal

# "My Little Muffins"
## Children's Toy Box

Why a muffin pan? Why *not* a muffin pan? When it comes to kids and having crazy, wild, and goofy fun—anything goes. But that isn't always what Mommy is thinking when she steps on spiky playthings in the middle of the night. Before *that* happens again, make a clean sweep through little junior and missy's bedroom to confiscate the guilty little playthings. Don't feel bad, because you're about to transform them into art. A standard muffin pan is equipped with twelve wonderfully roomy spaces to house everything from toothless smiles to action figures. Invite your child to help you create a playful wall piece that will hang nicely in their bedroom. However, don't forget to use the glue. You never know when the kids will have the urge to reclaim the toys, no matter how artfully they are arranged.

**Materials**

Standard muffin pan

5 or 6 small pictures of kids

Mini toys and candies

Party streamers

Spray paint

Construction paper

Foam board

Scalloped scissors

Picture-hanging attachment

Basic craft supplies (see page 17)

1) Clean the pan of debris. Spray paint in desired color in a well-ventilated area. Line the various muffin cups with construction paper.

2) Cut out pictures with scalloped scissors and glue a border from a crumpled party streamer around the edge. Using hot glue, adhere a small piece of foam board to the back of the pictures and mount into the muffin cups.

3) Take time to arrange the toys in the remaining cups until you find an assemblage that is balanced. Glue the items down and let dry. (See tip below).

4) Using industrial-strength craft glue, adhere a hanging attachment to the back.

**TIP**
Stick with industrial-strength craft glue when adhering items directly to the pan (hot glue will not bond properly).

**VARIATIONS**
• If you do not have a muffin pan, use another box that has many small compartments.
• Instead of school photos, take the children to a self-service photo booth at the mall. This will add even more whimsy to the box.

**Dimensions** 10 ½" X 14" (27 cm X 36 cm)        **Artist** Kathy Cano-Murillo (concept by Jenny Ignaszewski)

# CHAPTER 3

# Tributes to History and Culture

Every minute around the world, someone is taking part in a historical or cultural event. It could be as lighthearted as watching a World Series baseball game or attending a Hawaiian luau for the first time. It could also be as powerful as witnessing a birth or watching a breaking story unravel before our eyes on the morning news.

These are all nuggets of history and culture in the making. But the retelling of these nuggets can only be shared so many times before the details begin to become distorted or fade away. Ultimately, it's only a matter of time before our favorite lengthy anecdotes are trimmed back to quick glimpses. That's why it's so crucial to record these ties to the historical events of our lives—not only for our own use, but also for that of future family members.

Shadow boxes and shrines are a perfect way to incorporate our perspectives on world events and customs into lasting art assemblages. Even an item as simple as a ticket stub, an old photo, or a dated newspaper clipping will act as an essential centerpiece from which to build. Adding other associated objects, followed by writing about the experience on the back of the piece, then enhances the finished product.

The box or shrine will preserve your storytelling talent in all of its original glory. So when those memory lapses ultimately surface and you can't recall the details, you can then smile, relax, and let your original art piece be your guide.

Guidatta Pasta (Dedicace), 1950
Tate Gallery, London

**Artist** Joseph Cornell (1903 – 1972)

# Joseph Cornell
## by Paula Grasdal

Like the alchemist's dream of converting base metals into gold, assemblage artist Joseph Cornell transformed mundane objects into extraordinary poetic statements. After celebrating a career that spanned forty years, he is now considered one of the art world's modern masters.

In his imaginative world of creating message-bearing boxes, life's brief moments and littlest elements are transformed into creative worlds of their own—scraps of tulle and sequins conjure up the ballet, and a soap-bubble pipe paired with a map of the solar system create a playful link between bubbles and planets. Upon examining his many works, one can imagine Cornell meticulously working away in his basement studio late at night—concocting imaginary worlds and distilling memories.

Cornell became a memory himself when he passed away in 1972. But during his time on Earth, he was a reserved, contemplative person. He was considered a daydreaming loner who lived a quiet life in a small house in Queens, New York, which he shared with his mother and handicapped brother. The catalyst for his art career was Max Ernst's surrealist collage novel, *La Femme 100 Têtes,* which Cornell encountered at a gallery in New York City. Ernst's use of found objects and images inspired and liberated Cornell from the weight of traditional art forms such as painting or drawing. (Cornell had no formal art training.)

Cornell's first art objects were collages made from nineteenth-century engravings. They were exhibited in the early 1930s. A few years later, he discovered the medium of assemblage, which would occupy him for most of his remaining life.

He had a passion for collecting the contents for his art boxes. He often embarked on a train into Manhattan where he scavenged bookstores and secondhand shops in search of old maps, charts of the heavens, historical images, and natural history books. These outings, which he called "pilgrimages," also took place close to home at local five-and-dime stores. There he found modest yet valued trinkets such as marbles, glass

goblets, metal rings, and wood blocks. Other times, he rode his bicycle away from the urban landscape to gather bark, leaves, twigs, or moss. These outdoor materials ultimately found their way into his haunting *Owl* boxes of the 1940s and 1950s.

The imagery in Cornell's art boxes reflect a wide range of interests—from ballet to opera, Hollywood movies, French poetry, natural history, astronomy, and childhood pastimes. Each piece began as a single idea that was expanded to encompass related themes until a web of references was connected within each piece. Poetic juxtapositions such as the aviary and the game, the constellation and the European hotel, and the penny arcade and the Renaissance painting or starlet, were central to his artistic aesthetics. Themes reccurred in his boxes in various combinations.

Some of his boxes were devised with interactive features that included noise, as in the *Sand* boxes with loose flotsam and jetsam. Others revealed hidden contents, as did the drawers in the *Aviary* boxes. Victorian-era toys, including puppet theaters, optical devices, magic lanterns, and soap bubble sets, inspired many of his creations as well.

His detailed boxes symbolized how he felt about a particular subject or experience, and he lent them a dreamlike enchantment. They will forever resemble epiphanies or clear, transcendent moments captured by his imagination. His work embraced a pared-down simplicity that, like a visual poem, encapsulated a mood or a meaning.

Cornell's boxes are in numerous private and public collections including the Museum of Modern Art in New York and the Smithsonian Institution in Washington, D.C. His innovative approach to assemblages and shadow boxes influenced a whole generation of artists.

There are many reasons why Cornell's art has left a timeless impression. Perhaps one reason is because the viewer is able to assign meaning to the works that relates to his or her own inner world.

# Joseph Cornell Tribute Box

This assemblage pays tribute to Joseph Cornell, a master of constructing poetic worlds in miniature. By combining themes such as the aviary, French culture, and childhood games, this box is reminiscent of Cornell. The unassuming bird perched in the box represents the artist, who had a quiet exterior but a magical inner life.

**Materials**

Wood box

Game board or masonite panel

2" (5 cm) plywood circle

2 basswood strips, ½" × ⅛" × 12"
(1 cm × 3 mm × 30 cm)

Wood balls

Wood dowels

Wood for the frame

½" (1 cm)-thick balsa wood

Wood for the bird

Map of Paris

Postage stamps

Glass

Photocopy of a 6" × 2" (15 cm × 5 cm)
bird image

Foam core

Walnut-tone stain

Acrylic medium

Acrylic paints in burnt umber,
gold, and copper

Mat board

Sandpaper

Gesso

Basic craft supplies (see page 17)

Basic tools for making shadow boxes
(see page 19)

1) Lightly sand the wood box, wipe with a damp cloth, and paint with walnut stain. Cut a masonite or game panel 3" (8 cm) shorter than the box's inside length. Drill a random pattern of ½" (1 cm) holes in the panel (an old game called Labyrinth, which already had holes, was used here). Paint the box and panel with gesso and antique the surface with sandpaper.

2) Age a Paris map by rubbing on a little walnut stain. With acrylic medium, fix the map to the inside, back portion of the box. Glue two postage stamps to two tiny pieces of foam core and attach them to the map so they will be visible through the panel's holes. With wood glue, fix ½" (1 cm)-high wood strips to the bottom of the panel and glue the panel on top of the map. Decoupage part of the map onto a plywood circle and attach a stamp fragment in the center. Attach a hanging device on the back of the box.

3) Fix the bird image to the balsa with acrylic medium and carefully cut out the shape with a craft knife. Lightly sand the edges of the wood and paint the bird with acrylic paints (here, burnt umber mixed with metallic copper paint).

4) Cut two ⅛" (3 mm) dowels to the width of the box. Construct a chute for one of the balls by drilling two holes into two small pieces of bass wood and pushing narrow dowels into the holes. Paint the structure with gesso and attach inside the lower portion of the box. Paint a ½" (1 cm) dowel with gesso and place it vertically inside the box near the front. Paint three wood balls with metallic gold, then a wash of white, and glue onto the chute and the floor of the box with epoxy.

5) Make a frame from wood molding that overlaps the outside of the box; cut the molding to size and glue the sides to the bottom only (the top molding will be removable). Coat the frame with walnut stain. Dry and paint with gesso. Antique the surface with sandpaper.

6) Attach the bird and the wood circle with craft glue. With the back of the box resting on your work surface, place a sheet of glass on the front. Attach the frame by gluing the overhang to the bottom and sides of the box. Fix the top of the frame with screws.

**TIPS**
- When cutting through the balsa, work in layers for more control and a cleaner cut.
- Rub candle wax on areas of the stained wood before painting with the gesso. The waxed areas will release the paint more readily during the sanding stage.

**VARIATION**
Experiment with other Joseph Cornell themes such as palaces, observatories, European hotels, natural history, or ballet.

# **Colorful** Casitas

In Spanish, *casita* translates to "little house." But the meaning doesn't apply only to actual living spaces. Creating artistic *casitas* as colorful and ornamental wall shrines has become a respected and creative art form that can been seen in galleries as well as households throughout Mexico. These wall shrines are created from raw wood dollhouse furniture and then spiced up with south-of-the-border flair. Anyone who has traveled to Mexico has probably picked up a collection of inexpensive souvenirs and trinkets. All of these can be incorporated into a *casita* that features your favorite aspects of the ancient land.

**Materials**

Miniature dollhouse cabinet

Assorted Mexican images from newspapers, art books, magazines, postcards, postage stamps, food labels, loteria game pieces, or comic books

Mexican beer bottle caps

Mexican trinkets such as coins, bus tokens, matchbooks, mini pottery, medals, or milagros (Mexican miracle charms)

Embellishments: rhinestones, fabric roses, beads, glitter, crepe paper, or mini-cactus

Acrylic paints

Loose glitter

Dimensional squeeze paint

Water-based varnish

Sawtooth picture hanger

Basic craft supplies (see page 17)

1) Use a color copier to reduce images if necessary and then cut out all images.

2) Paint a base coat on the box in several colors.

3) Choose one larger image for the box's focal point. Use white glue to adhere it to the interior. Apply the other images to the box sides and top and to both sides of the doors. Outline the images with squeeze paint. Use a glue gun to attach trinkets around the box in a balanced matter.

4) Add loose embellishment items, glitter, and painted accents. Attach sawtooth picture hanger to the back of the box.

5) Apply a thin layer of varnish to preserve your box.

**TIP**
Pick one theme, such as Frida Kahlo or the Virgin of Guadalupe, to build upon, or create a casita that combines a variety of elements.

**Dimensions** 6" X 4" X 2" (15 cm X 10 cm X 5 cm)        **Artist** Kathy Cano-Murillo

# **World Series** Collectibles Box

Batter up! The year was 2001, and the Arizona Diamondbacks were considered the rookies of American baseball. After all, the bat-happy desert dwellers had been unified as a team for only four years. Enter the World Series. Decked out in purple and teal, the D-Backs found themselves brim to brim with longtime champs, the New York Yankees. Across the country, little respect was given to the new kids on the block. But by the time the edge-of-your-seat series rolled around to game seven, a new sense of credibility and pride radiated from the Phoenix dugout—especially when the Diamondbacks won the championship! Those fans lucky enough to get tickets have now enshrined their famous stubs as a priceless memory that will be cherished forever.

**Materials**

Shadow box with removable back panel

Ticket stub

Foam board

Cutouts of sports players

Small mementos from game

Mat frame

Sawtooth picture hanger

Acrylic paints

Stencil brush

Basic craft supplies (see page 17)

1) Remove the back panel from the box. Create a faux finish on the surface with a stencil brush and paints to match the team's colors. Cut a small piece of foam board about the size of a stick of gum and use a glue stick to attach it to the back of the ticket stub. Add a small accent item if desired.

2) Using the glue stick, add pictures of team players to the matt frame. Do not use any dimensional items, as the mat will not rest flat against the glass.

3) Lay the box flat on a table with the front facing down. Gently place glass inside box and then the mat frame. Run a bead of hot-glue around the edges to seal them.

4) Replace the back panel and repeat the sealing process. Add a sawtooth picture hanger to the back.

**TIP**

Do not use glue gun on the back of the ticket stub, as it will burn through to the other side.

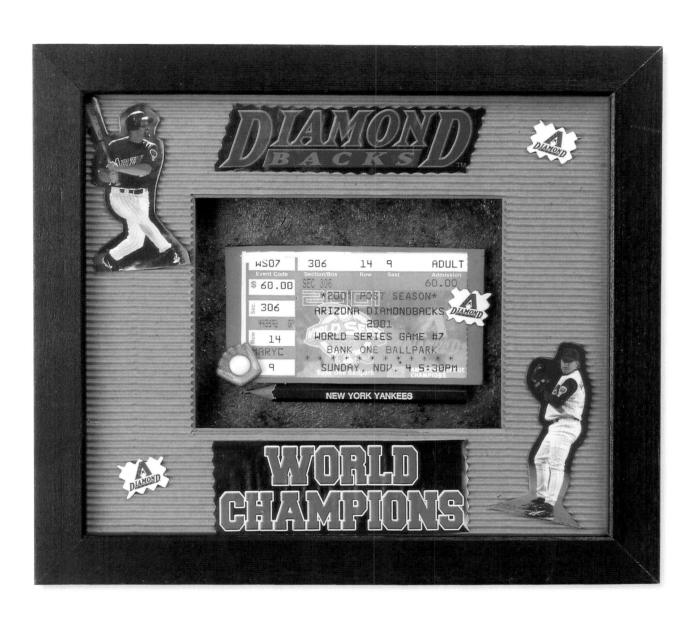

# **Blue** Elvis

Elvis may have left the building, but he lives on this shadow box—especially once the contents are sealed inside. This playful packaging radiates with all the burning love it took to create it. A hunky young Elvis is donning his legendary threads while fans cheer on his hip-swiveling, lip-quivering, hair-shaking performance. No wonder he's all shook up.

### Materials

6" × 9" (15 cm × 23 cm) shadow box with removable back panel

⅛" (3 mm)-thick sheet of balsa wood

photograph or color photocopy of Elvis Presley

6" (15 cm)-tall image of Elvis

3" × 5" (8 cm × 13 cm) image or sketch of a crown

Photocopy of audience or fan images

Acrylic paints in dark and light blue, white, black, yellow, pink, and silver

Silver bugle beads

24" (61 cm) string of Mardi Gras beads (or round yellow beads and beading string)

2 gold candles (birthday candles can be painted)

Assorted miniature artificial flowers

Thin, pliable wire for binding flowers

Decoupage medium

Water-based matte polyurethane

Low-tack masking tape

Sandpaper

Basic craft supplies (see page 17)

1) Cut out your Elvis head from the photocopy, including his neck (the head shown here is an image from an old calendar). Cut the body from the 6" (15 cm) Elvis image and position along with the head cutout on the balsa wood. Trace all around for an outline of the full body/head structure. Also cut out the crown and place separately on the balsa. Cut out both pieces with a craft knife. Go over the cutting line gently, a few times, to avoid splitting the fragile wood. Be sure all lines have been cut clear through before trying to extract the pieces.

2) Lightly sand the body and crown. Remove the back panel from the shadow box and wipe the box clean. To protect the box's glass inset while painting, tape strips of low-tack masking tape along the outer edges on both sides. Paint Elvis's shirt, jacket, and pants as shown in the photo. Paint the crown yellow, let dry, and then add silver trim around the edges. Prime the outside of the box with white paint and paint the interior light blue. Let dry. Apply a layer of water-based varnish to all surfaces but the glass. Remove the tape.

3) Attach the photo of Elvis's head to the wood cutout with craft glue. Glue silver bugle beads to the jacket to create the cuffs and lapels. Repeat for the collar and shirt seam. Cut out two short strips of balsa wood (about ¼" [5 mm] × 1" [3 cm]) and paint and glue them to the back of Elvis's feet for extra support.

4) To decorate the box's outside borders, use the decoupage medium to adhere images of your choice. This project features an audience from a concert performance. Apply a coat of decoupage to the covered box. When dry, apply one to two layers of polyurethane.

5) Gather two mini bundles of flowers. Use short lengths of wire to attach each bundle to a candle. The arrangement should stand independently.

6) To assemble the box, use craft glue to attach the crown to the piece of removable backing and set aside. Gently lay the box face down and use the hot-glue gun to attach the string of Mardi Gras beads around the interior, outlining the glass. The beads should touch the plastic but be glued to the inner sides of the box. Glue one candlestick in place, then glue Elvis in the center, followed by the last candlestick. Flip the box over and attach the back panel.

**TIP**
If your Elvis head faces the wrong direction, flop the body and template before marking.

**VARIATION**
Substitute freely: prop a mini-guitar in the corner and use found objects. Disassemble some rhinestone earrings or use glitter contact paper to cover your box.

Dimensions 6" X 9" (15 cm X 23 cm)          Artist Holly Harrison

# Tiki Tribute

The combination of crystal blue waters, sand-lined beaches, and towering palm trees can only mean one thing—the Hawaiian tropics. If it's been a while since you've encountered tiki territory, here is a crafty way to bring a bit of that exotic, sunny paradise into your humble dwelling. The island-friendly contents in this shadow box are composed of the usual fare of tropical treasures, but those who are lacking in leis or ukuleles need not worry. Many of these items can be found at the local party-supply or import store.

## Materials

20" × 21" (51 cm × 53 cm) piece of plywood

4 pieces of pine, 2 at 21" × 2" × 4" (53 cm × 5 cm × 10 cm) and 2 at 17" × 2" × 4" (43 cm × 5 cm × 10 cm)

Nails and hammer

Tiki or Hawaiian-themed wrapping paper

Hula girl postard with a mat frame

Ukulele

Tiki party favors

Male and female hula dancer dashboard ornaments

Tiki coasters

Cowrie and colored seashells

Hawaiian souvenirs: leis, coconut bank, statues, ornaments, nuts, and trinkets

Acrylic paints in teal, yellow, blue, and red

6" × 4" × 2" (15 cm × 10 cm × 5 cm) small window box

Sandpaper

Basic craft supplies (see page 17)

1) Sand all wood pieces. Assemble a frame using the four 2" × 4" (5 cm × 10 cm) pine pieces, and then securely nail the frame to the plywood to create a shadow box. Paint the interior and exterior in several layers of colors, letting dry between each layer. Repeat for the small window box. When dry, sand the edges of the box to show bring the bottom colors up.

2) Measure and cut a piece of wrapping paper to fit the interior area of the box. In a well-ventilated area, coat the interior panel with the spray adhesive. Gently place the paper to cover the area. Lift and reposition if needed.

3) Attach the small window box to the bottom left corner and glue small trinkets in each window. Attach the postcard and mat frame in the upper right corner of the box. Use the glue gun to add small, colored seashells to the mat frame. Attach the ukulele to the center of the scene by using industrial-strength craft glue. Repeat the process for the dashboard figures in the front right area.

4) To decorate the borders, add the tiki party favors, coasters, cowrie shells, and flowers in a balanced line.

5) Glue the coconut bank, tiki statue, and more flowers along the top of box.

6) Add the hanging attachment to the back of the box for display.

### TIPS
- Use industrial-strength craft glue for heavier items.
- Take time to arrange items to your liking and don't hesitate to let the embellishments extend beyond the borders of the box.
- Be patient. Let the items dry before you move on to the next step to prevent breakage.

### VARIATION
Incorporate personal mementos into the box's arrangement such as photos, menus, airline ticket stubs, and hotel stationary or shampoo bottles.

**Dimensions** 20" X 21" X 5" (51 cm X 53 cm X 13 cm)　　　　　**Artist** Kathy Cano-Murillo

# **Alien** Invasion!

The *War of the Worlds* comes to fruition with this tribute to campy space invaders. From flashy comic books to low budget B-movies, visions of the strange extraterrestrials creatures and the heroes who battle them are sure to prompt a goofy grin or two. In the outer limits of the sci-fi universe, nothing is scared, so we might as well indulge in our imagination and have fun. The truth may be out there, but only you can box it in.

## Materials

Chunky box with depth

Sci-fi comics books

Polymer clay

Alien and army figures

Toy spaceships

Jewels or crystals

Green felt

Wire hangers cut in strips

Silver paint

Assorted acrylic paints

Polyurethane varnish

Translucent glitter glue

Drill

Wire cutters

Basic craft supplies (see page 17)

1) Apply a base coat of acrylic paint in a color of choice to the entire box and decide on a horizontal or vertical presentation.

2) Cut out the images and separate them by size. Choose a larger picture for the side and interior panels and adhere them by using the decoupage method.

3) Create an alien figure for the center-piece of your scenario. Mold the head, body, hands, and feet from polymer clay. Poke holes in each piece so you can connect them later. Bake the clay according to package directions. Measure and snip pieces of the wire hanger to fit the proportions of the alien (two legs, two arms, and one longer piece for the body and head). Attach the body

parts to the wire with glue. Let dry, and then cover in silver paint. Add painted details to the face and body. Glue a crystal or other type of object in his hand.

4) Line the interior base of the box with the green felt. Glue the space-ship and alien in the box. Continue to add the remaining figures in a storytelling fashion.

5) On top of the box, drill a hole in the back-right corner and attach the "antenna" (piece of the wire hanger) with glue. Top it off with an alien head. Add other figures and/or jewels as well.

6) Cover the entire box with a layer of brush-on translucent glitter glue and varnish.

**TIP**

Add hanging UFOs from the ceiling of the box with string and glue. To make rocks for the landscape, break off chunks of Styrofoam and cover with a faux stone product.

**VARIATION**

Replace the standard shadow box with an old empty television set for an ultra retro, high-tech look. If you don't have access to a set, create a facade with cardboard and paint.

**Dimensions** 11" X 9" (28 cm X 23 cm)          **Artist** Patrick Murillo

# CHAPTER 4

# Tributes to Hopes and Dreams

Coordinating personal places and sacred spaces doesn't always involve what has happened in the past. Many times, the goal is to create a peaceful niche in which to meditate on what is to come. Shadow boxes and shrines are a wonderful avenue for shining a light on visions of the future.

For one person, sitting within a colorful, blooming garden is all it takes to become inspired by the gifts that the cycle of life has to offer. Another individual finds motivation in reaching their goals by honoring loved ones who have passed on. As children and teenagers, we playfully exhibited this kind of art right on our bedroom walls! Think of taped-up posters of movie or music idols, images torn from travel brochures of far off lands, book excerpts or magazine headlines with quirky sayings. Subconsciously, this process helped to shape who we were to become and the agenda we set for ourselves. Creating a shrine or a shadow box dedicated to our hopes and dreams is the same process, just a bit more conscious.

Another factor in creating these pieces is that they don't always have to be created for our own selves. Throughout life's journey, we will come across special people, who at a moment in time may need a lift in their self-esteem. Sometimes all it takes is an offering of a handmade gift with a positive message, one that embodies all the wondrous opportunities and adventures ahead.

No matter what the purpose, visualizing hopes and dreams through assemblage art is a surefire way to stay focused on the elements needed to enhance your—or someone else's—life.

Artist: Steve García

This shrine, titled *For the Lost*, was inspired by a conversation between the artist and his father about friends that had been killed in World War II as well as people who had lost a loved one in the war. This shrine wishes the best for the lost wherever they may be in life or in the afterlife and lets them know they will forever be in our hearts, thoughts, and prayers. It is made totally from cast and hand-built ceramics. The imagery is made of screen-printed ceramic materials that are fired into the glazes.

# Hopes and Dreams

So by now you've finished that shadow box that shows off your fancy Vegas vacation. And you've put the polishing touches on your arrangement of vintage frames set on the fireplace mantel. But how about dedicating a special area to focus on the future?

Incorporating a shadow box or shrine into your life for the sole purpose of motivation can lend feelings of inspiration and drive. It can be as simple as sticking to a healthy diet with the aid of wonderfully trim photos of you taped to a treadmill. At the opposite end, it could be as comprehensive as a having a wealth shrine that comes complete with three coins in a fountain.

California resident Lorraine Aho has devoted her professional life to this topic. She and her husband, Erik, launched SacredHome.com in 1997. The two of them travel the globe to bring culturally diverse and spiritually uplifting home décor to the masses. Aho credits the site's ten thousand hits a month to this day and age, where stressful events are thrust upon our busy, overcomplicated lives. People are yearning for peace. And Aho makes sure she practices what her products preach.

Her fervor for all things sacred began when she was young. She kept mementos, photos, and candles neatly arranged on her bedroom dresser. Back then, she had no idea her informal assemblages had an official name—what we now call shrines or altars. These days she is more than aware—she now has several corners appointed to her different aspirations and goals.

"I tend to group things in a *feng shui,* directional-type manner," she says. "I have a 'helpful people corner' that has pictures of my grandmothers to remind me of what kind of strong, beautiful women they were, and then I also have my 'success corner' to help our business to thrive. I have the first dollar we ever made, and my bulletin board is filled with quotes that really touch me. I even keep items on my desk that give me positive subliminal messages, like these power stones that say 'believe' or 'trust.' They all help me stay balanced with what is important to me."

She is not alone in her yearning for the good life. She is representative of just how many women create their very own special and intimate corners. Many of these are in non-traditional places, such as bathrooms, vanity dressers, gardens, and even kitchens.

The kitchen? Of course. After all, the kitchen is where it all happens. It's the room where we sort, prepare, cook, and eat our food. The process is nourishing not only to our bodies but also to our psyche. The spirit and mood that the cook embodies while preparing the meals makes a huge impact on its outcome. By having a cheery display of items that relay warmth and energy nearby—and a chef who embraces them—the delectable dishes will give the term "soul food" a whole new meaning.

Never underestimate shrines or shadow boxes as a means for encouragement in reaching your goals. Aho suggests beginning a "hopes and dreams" space by looking closely at the items in your house and separating the ones that make you feel happy and lighthearted. Clear a special area in which to display them, and add splashes of color to lighten the mood. Incorporate images or words that move you. Most importantly, take time each day to visit the area and absorb the reason why you created it in the first place. Keep in mind that these motivating spaces don't always have to be spiritual or serious. They can be happy, playful, or eccentric. Ultimately, the power from them won't come from the actual objects you place in the area, but more from what they mean to you. Only you will know what that entails. As for Aho, she knows exactly what her various corners represent.

"They bring me two things—roots and wings," says Aho. "I've got the roots of my grandmother and my sisters who help keep me grounded, and then I have my ethereal side. These are my collections of angels and such. They give me the wings that let me free my mind and let me be more spiritually aware."

# In Loving Memory
## Pocket Shrines

When a loved one passes away, the grieving process can be overwhelming. Aside from a multitude of memories, each living being leaves behind a unique imprint—not only in the lives of family and friends but also in the universe itself. These pocket shrines are affectionately created to embrace and elevate the features for which that person is most remembered. The rust depicts the passing of time and healing, and the contents represent the personality. Altogether, the completed mini masterpiece serves as a portable example of a beautiful person and all the hopes and dreams he or she left behind.

### Materials

Mint tin

Photo of loved one

Small items that relate to the individual's personality: dried flowers from the funeral, portions of letters, a snippet from a handkerchief, jewelry, a car key, food label, etc.

Miniature decorative items: beads, coins, flowers, pictures, colored pebbles, seashells, stamps, and tinsel

Small angel decorations

Rusting agent

Gold paint

Acrylic paint and/or glitter in assorted colors

Foam board

Basic craft supplies (see page 17)

1) Empty the mints from the tin and wipe clean. Apply the rusting agent to the inside and outside of the tin according to directions on package.

2) Glue the photo of your loved one inside the tin. Arrange items to your liking and then glue them in place. Use small pieces of foam board to elevate objects for a dimensional look.

3) Decorate the front of the box in the same fashion. Add paint and glitter for extra embellishment.

### TIPS
- Use glitter glue stick to add color to the objects.
- Let rust additive completely dry before gluing items to it.

### VARIATION
Instead of gluing objects, write a poem or letter to your loved one and attach it inside. Add a small music unit so a favorite song will play when a button is pushed.

In Loving Memory

*Gregorio Y. Ybarra*

Born
March 12, 1909
Sonora, Mexico

Entered into Rest
October 1, 2001
Phoenix, Arizona

**Dimensions** 4" X 2" X 1" (10 cm X 5 cm X 3 cm)     **Artist** Kathy Cano-Murillo

# **Garden Angel** Shrine

Gardens represent the beauty of life in the simplest of forms. Gorgeous flowers, towering trees, and scrumptious fruits and veggies all begin from a tiny seed that is nurtured and shaped through maturity. Together, these pristine plants act as a thriving botanical showpiece for any outdoor area. This cheerful shrine will add to the graceful allure with a touch of homemade charm. Not to mention, the guardian angel will happily watch over your pretty perennials to ensure that they blossom in a positive, ethereal environment. What a way to grow.

**Materials**

Wood window box

Floral foam

Wood lattice

Silk grapevine

Angel of choice

Miniature wood fencing

Various faux fruits and vegetables

Garden accessories such as gloves, mini shovel, seed packets, watering can, plant food, mini terra-cotta pots, and topiary

Outdoor acrylic paints

Stencils

Basic craft supplies (see page 17)

1) Fill the window box half way with floral foam. Insert a wooden lattice section upright into the foam in the back of the box. Lightly dab a dry paintbrush in the outdoor paint and lightly stroke it over the box and lattice. A light golden color was used here.

2) Lay the stencil on top of the front of the box. Use a stencil brush and a contrasting acrylic to fill in the stencil shape onto the box.

3) Weave several vines of silk grape leaves through the center and top of the lattice. Cross the vines to make an arch at the top of the shrine.

4) Place one magnificent angel at the center of the lattice. The angel in this project was made from a broom and raffia. Her halo is adorned with golden beads glued to a ribbon.

5) Trim the top edge of the window box with miniature wood fencing. Attach the flowers, vegetables, and seed packets in a random, balanced fashion.

**TIPS**
- Use floral wire to secure heavy objects to the lattice.
- Because your shrine will be outside, make sure your angel is made from materials that will withstand the elements.
- Keep it in a shaded area for the best preservation. Consider covering your shrine in plastic if you know it is going to rain.

# Voyage of Discovery Shrine

The term "far and away" never felt so wonderful. This shrine recalls the days when early explorers used the night sky to navigate their way toward distant lands. The theme parallels the mood of wonder and fascination that travelers experience in foreign countries. Peering through binoculars into the distance, you can imagine traveling to a Tuscan hill town or wherever your heart desires.

**Materials**

Photocopied images of a sundial, a sailboat, or an astronomical diagram

4" × 5½" × ½" (10 cm × 14 cm × 1 cm) piece of plywood

½" (1 cm)-wide basswood strip, 24" (61 cm) long

Wood clock case

Small wood box

Compass

Old binoculars

Silver egg cup

Two wood balls, 1" (3 cm) in diameter and 2" (5 cm) in diameter

Canvas board

Mat board

Aluminum embossing foil

Self-drying clay

Acrylic paints in dark silver and black

Gouache paints

Gesso

Acrylic matte medium

Paste wax

Burnt umber pigment

Oil of wintergreen

Cotton swab

Burnishing tool

Stylus

Basic craft supplies (see page 17)

Basic tools for making shadow boxes (see page 19)

1) Remove clock parts from the wood casing and sand the box to remove any varnish. Wipe clean with a damp cloth. Cut the basswood strips long enough to frame out the front of the small wood box. Using craft glue, adhere the wood strips together and attach to the opening of the box to create a frame. When glue has set, paint all box surfaces and the clock casing with three coats of gesso.

2) Cut canvas board to fit the inside back area of the shrine. Paint clouds on the upper portion of the board with gouache and glue the board in place with craft glue. Paint the world on the larger wooden ball with gouache. Push some self-drying clay into the egg cup to support a wooden ball. When the clay has dried, coat the top with black acrylic paint and glue the world onto the clay with epoxy.

3) Cut the plywood to fit inside the bottom of the shrine—the area here measures 4" × 5½" (10 cm × 14 cm). Stain one side of the plywood with watered-down gesso. Let dry. To transfer the image of the sundial (or other navigational image), tape the photocopy face down onto the gesso-coated wood and paint the back with oil of wintergreen. Burnish the image until it transfers onto the wood's surface. Allow the oil to dry and then lightly sand the image in areas for an antique effect. Glue

this piece of wood into the shrine ½" (1 cm) out from the back to create a support for the small box.

4) Tape the astronomical diagram on the aluminum embossing foil. On a soft surface, such as a magazine, trace the design with a stylus or a ballpoint pen to emboss the foil. Turn the foil over and lightly sand the surface. Patinate the embossed design with dark silver acrylic paint or wax, and paint other areas of the metal with gesso. Cut the foil to fit the inside back portion of the small box and attach with craft glue.

5) Paint the smaller wooden ball with black and dark silver acrylic paints. Using a fine-pointed brush, paint constellations onto the ball with gesso. Attach painted ball and the compass to the small box with epoxy glue. Attach the small box on top of the plywood inside the shrine.

6) Coat the back of the photocopied boat image with acrylic matte medium and press down onto a small piece of mat board. When the medium has dried, cut the boat image to fit inside binoculars or behind a magnifying lens. Tint the image with watered-down gouache and attach the boat behind the lens. Glue the egg cup and binoculars with epoxy and finish the outside of the shrine with paste wax tinted with burnt umber dry pigment.

**TIPS**
- Use a cotton swab to paint the back of the photocopy with oil of wintergreen. Make sure the tape does not cover any of the image to ensure a complete transfer.
- Look for old clocks, binoculars, and metal objects at thrift stores or flea markets.

Dimensions 14″ x 8″ x 4½″ (36 cm x 20 cm x 11 cm)      Artist Paula Grasdal

# Match Box Lapel Pins

Shadow boxes don't always take on the form of a wall hanging or table showpiece. The concept can be easily converted into a micro-masterpiece that will be the perfect accessory to any wardrobe. By transforming an ordinary matchbox into a lapel pin, you can add a dash of flash and flair to an overcoat, sweater, shirt, or hat.

**Materials**

Small matchbox base

Small photo to fit inside

Glitter

Micro beads

Miniature roses made of fabric or ribbon

Rhinestones

Assorted acrylic paints

Pin clasp

Foam board

Basic craft supplies (see page 17)

1) Paint the matchbox base in a desired color.

2) Trim the picture and glue a small piece of foam board to the back. Glue it inside the matchbox.

3) Trim the edges with glitter and micro beads. Add other small-scale embellishments such as miniature roses or rhinestones that will enhance the image.

4) Attach the pin clasp.

**TIP**
This project is most successful when several pins are made at one time. This allows for mixing and matching of decorations and pictures.

**VARIATIONS**
- Use textured trims, such as greenery, colored tissue, ribbon, or lace, to line the backs of the pins.
- Make a necklace or ornament by threading a string of satin cording through the pin clasp.

**Dimensions** 2" X 1½" (5 cm) X 4 cm)                    **Artist** Kathy Cano-Murillo

# A Soldier's Prayer Shrine

Throughout history, many American service personnel have brought along spiritual items with which to pray while stationed or fighting overseas. This portable, patriotic prayer shrine is small, quiet, and personalized to offer a soldier sanctuary and comfort. The center panel is tailored to the soldier's particular faith. With camouflage fabric and batting as the foundation, this lightweight piece comes with a family photo and includes two secret pockets to hold a rosary, a letter, or a memento. This inspirational shrine protects the most important ideas contained inside: duty to one's country and family bound by faith in God.

**Materials**

¼ yard (23 cm) camouflage fabric

¼ yard (23 cm) white cotton fabric

17" × 5" (43 cm × 13 cm) batting

Matching thread

Coordinating embroidery floss

Embroidery needles and hoop

Family photo and iron-on photo-transfer kit

Drawing pencil and white paper

2 small flag patches

3 buttons, ⅞" (2 cm) in diameter

Off-white dimensional squeeze paint for fabric

1) Wash and dry the fabrics. Cut two pieces of camouflage fabric to measure 19" × 7" (48 cm × 18 cm), and two pieces of white cotton to measure 5½" × 7" (14 cm × 18 cm). Cut another to measure 6" × 6¾" (15 cm × 17½ cm). On the center of the largest fabric rectangle, draw a cross in the center and a random camouflage pattern inside.

2) Set an embroidery hoop over the rectangle with the cross and embroider with satin stitch, French knots, or decorative stitching to fill. Fold ½" (1 cm) seam selvages around the edge of the piece. The fabric should now measure 5" × 5¾" (13 cm × 14½ cm). At the top of the 6" (15 cm) white fabric, finish edge with zigzag stitching. Fold under the ⅓" (1 cm) seam selvage on all edges. Embroider the outer edge of the fabric to form the border for the photo. Use an iron-on photo transfer, trimmed to fit the center of the panel. After the transfer has cooled, use squeeze paint to add a border around the photo, and let dry.

*(continued on page 86)*

**TIP**

Hand stitching and quilting adds a heartfelt element to the piece. Don't worry about getting everything straight and even—it's the thought that really counts in this piece. Iron in between steps to keep fabric flat and crisp.

**Dimensions** 18" X 6" (46 cm X 15 cm)                    **Artist** Anita Y. Mabante Leach

## A Soldier's Prayer Shrine—*continued*

3) Stack and center two flag patches on the remaining 6" (15 cm) white fabric. Fold ¼" (2 cm) selvages on the sides. By hand or machine, tuck and roll the top in by ¼" (2 cm); sew to finish. At the bottom, press a ½" (1 cm) seam selvage. Center the batting on the wrong side of camouflage piece. Baste around the edges to keep the batting in place. Center the embroidered crosspiece in middle of the right side of the batting-backed camouflage. Baste into place, tucking raw edges under. Place the flag piece to the left of the cross piece, placing the fabric ½" (1 cm) away from the center panel. Baste into place, tucking raw edges under. Place the photograph to the right of the cross panel, about ½" (1 cm) away. Baste into place, tucking raw edges under.

4) Sew the side seams, leaving the upper edge of the flag and photo panels free to form pockets. Knot and trim any loose threads. Place the remaining camouflage fabric, right sides together. Stitch ½" (1 cm) seams all around, leaving 6" (15 cm) at bottom. Trim seams and corners. Turn the piece right side out and iron. Hand stitch a 6" (15 cm) hole at the bottom to close. Flip the quilted piece over. On the outer left edge (flags are on the flip side), machine or hand stitch three 1" (3 cm)-wide buttonholes, spaced evenly. Fold the piece in thirds, positioning buttonholes. Mark. Sew buttons, taking care not to sew through the photo on the flip side.

### VARIATIONS
- Choose camouflage that matches the solder's uniform.
- Sew on appropriate insignias, if desired.

# Wishful Thinking:
## Inspirations for the Creative Cook

Not everyone is a gourmet cook. Sure, cookbooks can help, but no matter how many times the same food formula is concocted, it never comes out quite the same. Here's an idea for the blooming chef who could use a bit of positive inspiration in the kitchen. Think of it as a calorie-free, artistic recipe that makes playing with your food almost as fun as eating it. And unlike the directions in a cookbook, this project encourages you to alter the ingredients as you wish.

**Materials**

8½" × 8½" (22 cm × 22 cm) shadow box with border

Acrylic paints in fuchsia, teal, and orange

Sandpaper

Miniature kitchen gadgets

Dry foods: pinto beans, rice, chilies, coffee beans, or pasta

Miniature faux fruits and vegetables

10 small assorted food-related magnets

4 bottle caps

Basic craft supplies (see page 17)

1) Apply an even base coat of teal paint to the entire box. Let dry and repeat the process to the border by adding layers of orange and fuchsia. When dry, lightly sand the surface, edges, and corners to bring out the colors from underneath.

2) Arrange the kitchen gadgets to the center of the box and adhere with a hot-glue gun.

3) Paint the insides of the bottle caps and fill with coffee beans.

4) To decorate the border, attach the largest items first in a balanced fashion. Glue a bottle cap in each corner. Add the colorful magnets, leaving enough room to insert the fruit and vegetables in between. Add rows of pinto beans around the inside and outside frames of the box.

**VARIATION**

A variation is to attach the kitchen gadgets to the border and the magnets and miniature fruits and vegetables to the center. This project can be altered to fit any personality such as a coffee, Italian, retro, or cocktail theme.

**Dimensions** 8 ½" x 8 ½" (22 cm x 22 cm)     **Artist** Kathy Cano-Murillo

# Kwanzaa Keepsake Box

A celebration of family, community, and culture are the foundations of Kwanzaa, an uplifting and spiritually empowering African-American holiday. The weeklong event embraces and promotes *Nguzo Saba* or "the seven principles" of self-improvement and reflection: unity, self-determination, collective work and responsibility, cooperative economics, purpose, creativity, and faith. A large part of Kwanzaa are the festive altars in red, black, and green that are assembled in the home. These loving installations showcase symbolic African items including fruits, baskets, fabrics, harvest symbols, and artwork. Seven candles stand tall in the center—one for each day and principle.

**Materials**

4½" × 4½" (11 cm × 11 cm) shadow box

5" × 5" (13 cm × 13 cm) piece of red silk or Kwanzaa fabric

Black and yellow foam board

Kwanzaa postage stamp

4 strips of yellow leather, 4" (10 cm) each

4 small cowrie shells

Green spray paint

Acrylic paints in red, blue, and black

Fabric glue stick and hot-glue gun

Head pin

Brush-on varnish

Basic craft supplies (see page 17)

1) Disassemble the shadow box. In a well-ventilated area, spray paint the frame green and let dry.

2) Use a glue stick to adhere the fabric to the back panel of the box. Snip the corners of the fabric and fold neatly over the edges.

3) Cut a 2½" × 1½" (6 cm × 4 cm) piece of the yellow foam board and glue horizontally in the panel center. Cut a 1¼" × 1" (3½ cm × 3 cm) piece of the black foam board and glue horizontally in the center of the yellow panel. Place the postage stamp in the center of the black piece.

4) Glue the leather strips in the frame center on all sides. Paint the outer area red. Dip a head pin in black paint and draw primitive-looking designs along the border. Let dry and brush on the varnish. Add a cowrie shell to each corner.

5) Assemble the box when all pieces are completely cured. Attach a saw-tooth picture hanger on the back.

**TIP**
Use scalloped shears to give your foam board's edge a finished look.

**VARIATION**
The stamp can be replaced with small, African artifacts or images (see http://www.officialkwanzaawebsite.org).

# CHAPTER 5

# Sharing Celebrations

Have you ever felt so overjoyed about an accomplishment or experience that you just absolutely had to share it with the world? Welcome to the celebrations chapter. This is the area of the book that is dedicated to all things that deserve a toast of the bubbly and a toss of glittery confetti. It's all about being thankful for the little things in life that make us smile, laugh, giggle and even shed tears of joy.

Passionate romance, guilty pleasures, furry friends, and dancing puppets are just a few of the featured projects. Hopefully they will motivate you to ponder the tokens in life that bring you bountiful bliss. Rule number one: Let serendipity be your guide. Collect and apply articles that exude your blushing excitement and overwhelming passion for the topic.

As with all interactive art pieces, composition is an important element. But when it comes to celebratory subjects, it's not the *only* element. It's all about the party. The top objective is to unite all the festive aspects, no matter how outlandish they may seem. Make room for all sorts of trinkets and goodies without passing judgment.

From gilded angels to bingo cards, you'll see the ultimate of examples within the next few pages. Just keep in mind that the meaning of the word *celebration* lies in the eye of the beholder.

# El Día de los Muertos

No bones about it, *El Día de los Muertos* (The Day of the Dead) is not your ordinary fiesta. Held on Oct. 31 through November 2, it's a festive tradition where the spirits of the dead are actually the life of the party. This cherished south-of-the-border holiday not only honors the dearly departed, but also invites them back home for a soirée, meal, dance, and maybe even a shot of tequila.

In Mexico the concept of dying is not something to be feared. Instead it is respected and acknowledged as part of the wondrous cycle of life. Like all human beings, these Mexican families and friends are saddened when their loved ones pass on, but they use *El Día de los Muertos* as a way to rejoice over their loved one's journey on Earth and the beginning of a new one in the afterlife. The holiday also presents an opportunity to find personal closure after the loss.

Chicano artist Zarco Guerrero has been celebrating *El Día de los Muertos* since he was a child. He has his own interpretation on the meaning. "Death is a universal phenomena," he says. "No other culture celebrates death as extravagantly and/or elaborately as Mexico. It is an aspect of Mexican philosophy that is lacking in the American culture—a positive way to mourn the dead while honoring our indigenous past."

At first you might ask, "Why all the scary skeletons?" It only takes a moment to notice that "scary" has nothing to do with it. These skeletons are portrayed as happy and silly as a reminder that the spirit is eternally alive and well. "The biggest misconception is that it's macabre, pagan, or occult," he says. "Or that Chicanos and Mexicans are obsessed with death. Actually our obsession is with celebrating life and art."

For *El Día de los Muertos,* Guerrero, his wife, and their three children assemble several artistic *ofrendas* (altars) in their home as a way to show gratitude to their ancestors. Each year brings a new theme and message to reflect recent events and to honor important community figures that have passed on.

Despite the title of the holiday, the occasion actually lasts three days rather than just one. The first day is dedicated to infants and youngsters who have died. Beginning at noon on October 31, the living children set out paths of fragrant marigolds to invite the smaller souls into their homes. There, a beautiful altar with a hot meal, sentimental trinkets, and toys awaits them. Twenty-four hours later, at noon, the *angelitos* (little angels) return to the afterlife and preparations are made for the adult spirits to arrive and stay for the following twenty-four hours, until noon on November 2. Within that time frame, a jubilant community procession that includes skeleton stilt walkers, strolling musicians, art displays, and food booths is presented. In addition, like the Guerreros, families in the villages create their own ornate *ofrendas* in their living rooms or at specific gravesites.

When making a Day of the Dead altar or *ofrenda,* the idea is to combine the traditional elements listed below with some commonplace objects as well as items specifically enjoyed by the spirit that is being celebrated. Examples of common ingredients include flowers, candles, candy, coins, letters, Christmas lights, religious relics, pictures, a glass of water, a bottle of soda, beer, or spirits, coffee, chocolate, cigarettes, tamales, cigars. (The spirits are not really expected to eat the food; it is there to make them feel welcome if they do come to visit.)

It is the little personable details that distinguish the altar. Items relating to hobbies and passions—baseball cards, favorite magazines, paintbrushes, books, knitting needles—anything goes.

Overall, *El Día de los Muertos* is a joyous but also serious matter. Many believe the dead will become sad or angry if their families do not revere their spirit during this holiday and, in turn, will respond by bringing misfortune or bad luck. Break out with the sugar skulls, quick!

The following is an overview of the traditional elements of a Day of the Dead *ofrenda,* or altar. (See page 123 for information on where to locate some of these items.)

**Pan de muertos:** This golden, sweetened "bread of the dead" is baked in round loaves or skull shapes.

**Papel picado:** Mexican tissue-paper banners that are folded and then intricately cut by hand into whimsical scenarios. The panels are then strung together and hung above the altar.

**Copal:** This incense clears the path for spirits to find their way to their former homes.

**Zempasuchitl:** These are freshly cut marigolds flowers. The Aztecs believed the orange petals symbolized death and that the scent permeates through the air and acts as an invitation for the spirits to return to their grave. It is also known as "the flower with four hundred lives."

**Calaveras de alfeñique:** If this seems like an impossible word to pronounce, no fear. "Sugar skulls" will suffice. The message is bittersweet—the sugar represents the sweetness of life, and the skull represents the sadness of death. These playful pieces look good enough to eat. And they most certainly are. Molded from a homemade sugar paste, they are then decorated with icing, glitter, and foil.

**Calaveras and calacas:** These whimsical renditions of skulls and skeletons are used in many forms of artwork, music, poems, toys, and mini shadow boxes.

**La Catrina:** Mexican artist José Guadalupe Posada (1852 – 1913) creaeted this timeless, captivating image. He modeled this fancy lady after the upper-class French women of the early 1900s.

Just remember, not all Day of the Dead shrines have to be assembled in the expected format and with the traditional decorations. As with all types of shrines, a person can create an altar to their liking with or without all of the Mexican additives.

Artist: Patrick Murillo

Shadow boxes and whimsical scenes are a joyous part of the festivities that surround *El Dia de los Muertos.* This box depicts a comical shoeshine scenario. It was made from wood, clay, wire, and found objects.

# Desert Moon Dancer
## Shadow Box

It's a starry night in the middle of the prickly Southwest, and one can only imagine the festive activities that take place. Perhaps a whimsical desert dweller such as this celebrates with a dance to the shake of a rattle. This colorful box serves double duty as a puppet show. Pull the string to make your creature dance among the cacti.

### Materials

10" × 12" (25 cm × 30 cm) shadow box

Thin sheet of basswood

28-gauge wire

Nippers

10" (25 cm)-long dowel, ³⁄₁₆" (4½ mm) in diameter

4 pieces of carpet thread, each 16" (41 cm) long

Cardboard

Acrylic paint

Assorted beads

Water-based varnish

Small nails

Drill

Sandpaper

Picture-hanging hardware

Basic craft supplies (see page 17)

1) Sketch a façade that will frame the box. Trace the pattern on the basswood, and cut out. Repeat the process for a cactus, moon, and other desired decorative shapes. Cut them out with a jigsaw.

2) For the dancer: Sketch a pattern of body pieces onto the basswood that will make up the dancer. One piece will be the head and body. Two pieces are needed for each arm and each leg. There will be nine pieces to the dancer. Cut out the shapes with a band or scroll saw. Sand edges smooth, and paint a base coat.

3) Add detail to the cut-out shapes with whimsical painted designs. Set aside to dry. Paint the box's interior, exterior, and façade. Let dry. Apply a coat of water-based varnish.

4) To assemble the dancer, use a small drill bit to connect the body parts. The top of each arm and leg will require two holes side by side—one each for the wire and the pull string. Use wire to connect the arms and legs to the body, keeping the pieces loose. Tie a piece of carpet thread to the top of each arm and leg. Let the

excess hang down. Glue the dowel to the back of the dancer for support. Do not trim the excess dowel.

5) Drill two ³⁄₁₆" (4½ mm) holes at bottom of the box (one in center, the other directly behind it). One hole is for the pull string; the other is to insert the dowel holding the dancer.

6) Attach the front with small nails. Using wood or hot glue, choose, arrange, and then attach some of the cutout shapes to the interior of the box. Adhere small pieces of cardboard to the backs of the shapes with hot glue. Glue the remaining cutouts around the façade to cover the nails.

7) To attach the dancer, apply a bead of hot glue to the middle of the dancer's dowel. Going in through the front of the box, insert the dowel down into back-drilled hole. Thread the pull string through the front hole.

8) Thread beads onto the pull string for weight, then tie a knot to keep beads in place. Attach the picture-hanging hardware to back of box.

### TIPS
- For easier cutting, substitute cardboard or foam board for balsa wood.
- For faster preparation, purchase precut shapes at the craft store.

**Dimensions** 10" X 12" (25 cm X 30 cm)          **Artist** Kelly Hale

# American Pop Shrine

Worn edges, faded patriotic hues, and a hint of cozy hominess is what much of American folk art is all about. Sleek hairdos, glamorous jobs, and toothy smiles are what old Hollywood was all about. The two worlds collide in this table shrine that celebrates past eras and unfading patriotism.

## Materials

Wine crate

Two 4" × 6" (10 cm × 15 cm) wood boxes

Retro Hollywood photos, postcards, and magnets

Pop culture collectables: election pins, miniature food items, and vintage toys

Wood shapes in rectangles, stars, and hearts

Ribbon

String of blue beads

Crocheted doily

Standing photo holder

Acrylic paints in red, white, and blue

Sandpaper

Assorted adhesives

Scalloped scissors

Foam board

Highlighter pens

Basic craft supplies (see page 17)

1) Paint all areas of the wine crate and wood boxes in layers of red, then white, then blue, letting colors dry between each coat. When dry, sand the boxes to give them an aged look. Follow the same procedure for the wood shapes.

2) Cut dime-sized pieces of foam board. Trim the photos with the scalloped scissors and glue a piece of the foam board to the backs. If using black-and-white photos, add color with highlighter pens.

3) Sort items by shape. Rest the wine crate horizontally and glue a wood box in each corner. Glue the photo holder in the center of the box and use the doily to cover the base. Choose one photo to go in the stand. Adhere the other photos, postcards, and pins in a balanced manner to the back panel of the box.

4) Find items to rest inside and on top of the wood boxes. Using fishing line or string, attach dangling items to the top of the wine crate. Attach several eye-fetching items to the top of the wine crate and glue the string of beads along the front for the final touch.

**TIP**

Look in card shops for postcards of old movies or at yard sales for old magazines.

**VARIATION**

Instead of movie-related items, adjust the American pop theme to your liking by incorporating sports, toys, patriotic dolls, or other themes.

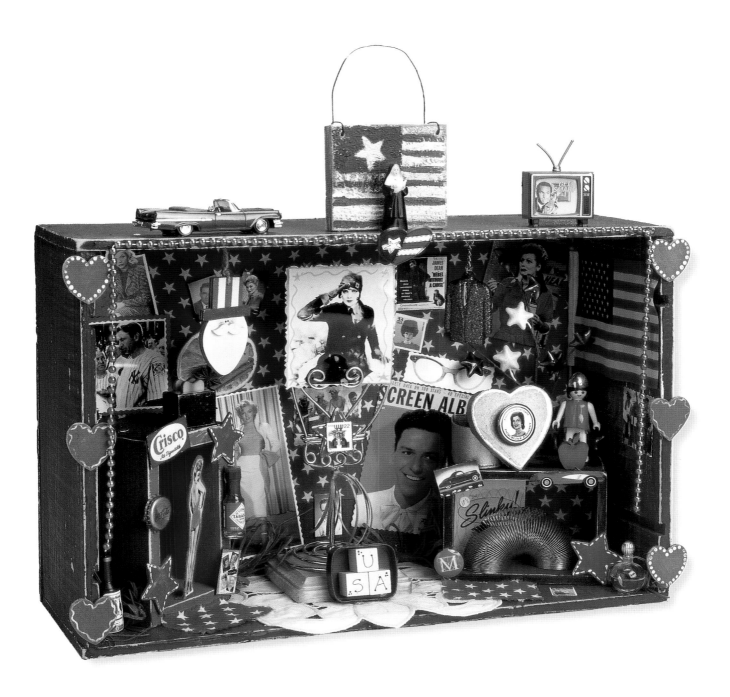

**Dimensions** 13" x 20" x 7" (33 cm x 51 cm x 18 cm)

**Artist** Kathy Cano-Murillo

# **Classic Romance** Shadow Box

A long-term romantic relationship is a gift to be celebrated and cherished. The natural progression of flirting, blushing, tickling, and kissing is usually accompanied with a fair share of sentimental hardware. You know the list—wine glasses, gourmet chocolates, candlelit dinners, remote vacations, and, with any luck, fresh-cut flowers. Although the romantic memories alone serve as the real milestones of success, the treasured keepsakes are just as priceless. A shadow box is a wonderful way to display the various events and travels of your romance. For those who have collected, cherished, and safely "tucked away" sacred items, this project is the perfect opportunity to bring them out to share. By arranging them in mini vignettes, they will make for one-of-a-kind visual journey of love and devotion.

**Materials**

Wooden shadow box with multiple windows

Collection of personal romantic treasures

Small romance-themed objects such as candles, wine, chocolate, love letters, flowers, hearts

4 to 5 yards (3¼ to 4 meters) tulle

Small crocheted or paper doilies or wrapping paper

Ribbon

Costume pearls

Miniature gift-wrapped boxes

Hot-glue gun

Picture-hanging hardware

Basic craft supplies (see page 17)

1) Work with your treasures and place them into small groupings. Sort them by event, color, or size and then fit them together in each window to create a small vignette. Let each window tell a short story of your romance.

2) Before gluing, assemble and rearrange objects in the windows in a balanced and appealing fashion. Line the bottoms of windows with doilies or wrapping paper.

3) Use the hot-glue gun to adhere the pieces. Work slowly, one window at a time.

4) Once all the windows are complete, finish off the box by adding ribbon or tulle around the edges.

5) Attach the hanging hardware to the back.

**TIP**
Stickers and pictures from gift cards work well for adding visuals to the backs of the windows. Cover the box in glass to preserve items.

**VARIATION**
Arrange objects in the chronological order of your relationship.

**Dimensions** 12" X 18" (30 cm X 46 cm)

**Artist** Michelle Zecchini Cano

# El Día de los Muertos Pet Altar

This particular *ofrenda,* or altar, is truly for the dogs. It's also meant for cats, turtles, birds, fish, and all our other friends of the animal kingdom. It contains all the yummy ingredients to lure the critters and creatures back home in style—rhinestone collar and all. If you like your altar, don't feel you have to take it down after *El Día de los Muertos* has passed. If it makes you happy, keep it up all year round. (See page 94 for more information on *El Día de los Muertos* altars.)

## Materials

22" × 7" (56 cm × 18 cm)-thick piece of plywood

3 pine boards, 22" × 2" × 4" (56 cm × 5 cm × 10 cm)

Silk vines or live greenery

Yellow and orange tissue paper flowers or fresh marigolds

Photos in assorted sizes of a beloved pet

Animal figures and toys

Mini candles

Dried sage, *copal* (see page 95), or incense

Feathers

*Papel picado*/tissue paper banners (see page 95)

Pet collars, pet food, identification tags

*El Día de los Muertos* objects such as sugar skulls, happy figures, or maracas (see page 95)

Painted bottle to hold flowers

Hammer and assorted nails

Acrylic paints

Polymer clay

Basic craft supplies (see page 17)

1) Attach two of the pine boards to create a flat base that measures 8" (20 cm) deep and 22" (56 cm) long. Attach the third board on top at the rear of the base for a tiered effect. The third board should be aligned evenly with the back of the base. Attach the plywood upright to the back of the base. Paint the entire surface in bright colors of choice.

2) Using the hot-glue gun, attach the greenery around the border of the plywood and along the bottom of the shelves. Add the flowers throughout the leaves.

3) Choose a photo to be the centerpiece of the altar and glue it to the center of the plywood. Line the top of the photo with a pet collar and glue smaller pictures and trinkets surrounding it.

4) Fill the shelves with happy mementos of your beloved pet and other related decorative objects.

5) Create *muertos* skulls with polymer clay. Bake according to the package directions. Then paint them and attach to the shelves borders. Add ribbons, *papel picado,* or other embellishments.

**TIP**
Do not glue items to the shelves so that items may be rearranged or replaced from year to year.

**VARIATION**
Instead of building an altar from scratch, use a wine crate or other type of portable box. Before lighting candles, make sure they are nowhere near any flammable items and never leave the lit candles unattended. Add Christmas lights for extra flair.

**Dimensions** 7" X 22" X 8" (18 cm X 56 cm X 20 cm)          **Artist** Kathy Cano-Murillo

# New Orleans Bingo
## Angel Shrine Box

Gumbo or gifts, New Orleans is the ultimate hot spot for robust flavor and extreme fun. During Carnival and Mardi Gras, the streets are continuously overflowing with visitors decked out in outlandish attire to match their bold, in-your-face personalities. Much like this shrine box. Even if the party scene is not your style, the Big Easy has plenty of other aspects in which to partake. Zydeco tunes, Cajun cooking, and intriguing landmarks are all worthy of incorporating into a gorgeous and gaudy shrine that also functions as a box to stash extra goodies.

**Materials**

Wooden cigar or jewelry box

Beads in assorted colors, shapes, and sizes

Pieces of vintage jewelry

Mini mirror pieces

Found objects, such as crosses, angels, doll parts, rubber crawfish, pictures, faux flowers, and coins

Bingo cards, cut up

Loose glitter

Glitter glue

Fabric

Sandpaper

Acrylic paints

Brush-on, water-based varnish

White craft glue

Strong cement glue

Basic craft supplies (see page 17)

1) Lightly sand the entire box and apply two to three layers of paint in a desired color. Let dry. Brush on a coat of varnish to seal the paint.

2) Arrange the pictures and objects to find a balanced and appealing look before gluing.

3) Choose one picture that will become one of the main focal points of your box and decorate it with decoupage. Continue to add remaining pictures all around the box, making sure that all edges are tightly adhered. When finished, coat the pictures with a layer of the varnish and let dry. Outline the edges of the pictures with glitter glue. Add sparkle to the edges by applying white craft glue and then quickly sprinkling on loose glitter.

4) Apply the found objects with the cement glue. Apply dashes of glitter glue as a finishing touch.

5) Line the inside of the box with fabric or more decoupage art.

**TIPS**
- Glitter may be applied under or on top of the paint for an ultratextured effect.
- Do not apply varnish anywhere near the inside edges of the box or the top and bottom will become glued together.
- Sand the edges of the mirror pieces to prevent accidental skin cuts.
- Use tweezers to apply small objects.

**VARIATIONS**
- Stencil or paint designs on the inside of the box.
- Glue a personal photo from your trip on the inside lid and decorate around it.

**Dimensions** 8½" X 11" (22 cm X 28 cm)

**Artist** Jean Siderio

# Anniversary Box

Roses, chocolates, and champagne may be a traditional method for honoring a wedding anniversary, but an artsy alternative is just as meaningful. Large, colorful leaves and pieces of textured birch bark were gathered during a nature walk to create the concept's foundation. Delicate, gold paper decoupage lines the box inside to accentuate the vibrant leaves. Nestled inside is another box that contains a silver heart and a loving message written on a fragment of birch bark. The dictionary pages on the lid display specially selected words such as astronomy, a passion of the artist's husband.

**Materials**

Box with lid

Old dictionary or photocopied dictionary pages

Pressed leaves

Birch bark

Moss

Matchbox

Heart charm

Gold paper

Acrylic matte medium

Acrylic paint in burnt umber

Staples and staple gun

White gel pen

Basic craft supplies (see page 17)

1) Create a decoupage effect to the box's lid by applying the gold paper and dictionary pages with acrylic medium. Age the papers with an antiquing glaze made from burnt umber acrylic paint and acrylic medium. Attach a pressed leaf to the center of the lid with craft glue and brush a protective coat of acrylic medium over the entire surface. Line the inside of the box with gold paper using the same method.

2) With acrylic medium layer the gold paper onto the inner and outer areas of the matchbox. Attach a tiny, pressed leaf to the lid with craft glue and arrange moss around the inside edge of the box. With epoxy, glue the heart milagro into the box so it is framed by the moss.

3) Write a message with a white gel pen on a tiny strip of birch bark and place it in the matchbox. Write the anniversary date on another piece of birch bark and glue it inside the box.

4) Arrange birch bark on the inside of the lid and attach with craft glue. Weigh the bark down as the glue sets. Add a few staples along one edge of the birch bark composition.

5) Fill the box with pressed autumn leaves. Add the tiny matchbox to complete.

**TIPS**
- Press the leaves between sheets of newsprint and layers of cardboard weighted with plywood. Change the newsprint every day for two weeks until the leaves are dry.
- To speed up the drying process, iron the leaves between sheets of newsprint.

**VARIATION**
This box could work for any season; try pressing flowers in the spring or summer as an alternative to the leaves or try making a winter box with silver paper and painted white twigs.

**Dimensions** 1 ½" X 8" X 8" (4 cm X 20 cm X 20 cm)          **Artist** Paula Grasdal

# **Whimsical** Angel Box

Although many feel they have an angel on their shoulder, it's always nice to be able to see it every once and a while. It's then we realize that each individual's perception of cherubs and ethereal guardians are vast as the dreams they yearn for. Bring an angel to life with this whimsical and cheery box that is easily assembled with a variety of basic craft supplies. Not to mention, a small amount of little divine intervention.

**Materials**

8½" × 8½" (22 cm × 22 cm) shadow box with border

Wood or ceramic angel head

Acrylic paints in patina blue, patina green, bronze, silver, and fuchsia

Polymer clay in green, yellow, and pink

Roll of lightweight silver and bronze tin

Gift wrap with angel and floral designs

Chunky 4" (10 cm) wood heart

Assorted rhinestones

Angel and heart charms

Sea sponge

White craft glue

Industrial-strength craft glue

Brush-on, water-based varnish

Scalloped scissors

Green and gold squeeze glitter

Basic craft supplies (see page 17)

1) Create a faux finish by layering colors of paints with the sea sponge. Use a bluish tone for the inside of the box and a pink one for the border. Paint a base coat on the angel head and then add detail with the assorted colors. Use your finger to lightly rub on bronze trim. Turn the box on the diagonal and glue the angel at the top. Paint the wood heart bronze and glue it inside the bottom corner of the box.

2) Cut out the flower, heart, and angel shapes from wrapping paper and apply with with white glue for a decoupage effect (flowers around the border and above the wood heart, angels in the inside corners). Outline with the squeeze glitter.

3) Make eleven clay roses (eight yellow and three pink) with leaves from the polymer clay. To make roses, form a pea-sized ball and pinch the bottom. Use craft knife to cut layers of petals and bend them back. To make leaves, flatten a piece of green clay and cut leaf shapes with a craft knife. Glue yellow roses in pairs around the border, and the remaining pink flowers on the wood heart. Add highlights with green, fuchsia, and bronze paint.

4) Add rhinestones, angel, and heart charms as accents throughout the box.

5) Cut four 8" (20 cm) strips of silver tin using scalloped scissors. Emboss designs by etching designs into the tin with a sharp pencil. Glue to the outer frame. Cut four 2" (5 cm) squares of bronze tin for corners. (Use care when handling tin, as edges may be sharp.)

6) Add detail to the edges of the box with thin lines of silver and bronze paint. Add a thin layer of varnish for protection.

**Dimensions** 8 ½" X 8 ½" (22 cm X 22 cm)

**Artist** Kathy Cano-Murillo

# Gallery

For many people, building multilayered shrines and elaborate shadow boxes isn't a one-time effort. There is a wealth of multitalented crafts artists across the world that uses this art form as a central part of their creative livelihood. This chapter features a handful of them. The carefully constructed installations come equipped with a social message or an underlying theme—sometimes serious, sometimes amusing, but always awesome and intriguing.

After tackling an initial shrine or wall box, you may feel compelled to take on a larger artistic investment. Perhaps one of these works will lend insight into the vast amount of resources. Within the next few pages you will discover extreme imagination in action that includes, but is not limited to, a Chinese war hero, a Jesus on wheels, a perspective on the afterlife, a weathervane, Madonna, and an animated Parisian café.

Consider these prestigious projects to be your launching pad into the world of magnificent altars and assemblages. You have been warned.

# Altar to Ancestral Spirits

This Buddhalike altar was created to petition the ancestral spirits for their supernatural assistance on Earth. Assisting the artist with her creation was a Mexican herbalist and healer who prepared the herbal packets within the assemblage. Traditionally, the happy Buddha stands for wisdom, purity, and compassion. But in this eccentric art piece, those elements are enhanced by a wild collection of novelties, found objects and obscure trinkets. Using an oversized terra-cotta saucer as the foundation, the artist playfully, yet spiritually incorporated her personality into her work. Ultimately, this bohemian Buddha will serve as a tangible reflection of the artist's own positive energy and personal, meaningful tribute to her ancestors.

**Artist** Nancy Nenad

# Memento Mori Altar

**Artist** Tisza Jaurique

The artist created a serious and respectful altar to the acknowledgment of death as part of the life cycle. Memento Mori is a concept that dates back to the Renaissance when illness and war claimed the lives of many innocent people. As a result, many artists of the era began to incorporate skulls into paintings, carvings and statues as a symbol of mortality—and a reminder that life must be cherished. This altar was created in a mixed media format from glitter, mirrors, glass, plastic, metal, and found objects.

# Kuan Kung Prosperity Shrine

**Artist** Marcus K. Zilliox

This elaborate altar was created to honor the ancient spirit of Kuan Kung—a wise, highly intelligent, and extremely stern warrior and businessman. Kuan Kung is known as the Chinese god of war and business, and statues of him are often found at the entrances of Chinese establishments. His fierce imagery confirms the belief that he serves as the guardian and protector of warriors, politicians, and business leaders. In the world of *feng shui*, it is recommended to place a statue or shrine to Kuan Kung in the northwest corner of your home, facing the front door, to maintain peace and harmony while protecting your sacred space from negative energy that may enter. The artist created this shrine by utilizing a variety of mediums including paint, metal, plastic, wood, fabric, and various found objects.

# The Ultimate RV Shrine

**Artist** Ralph "Mr. Shrine" Wilson

In the world of art, everything has a double meaning. Enter this RV—as in Religious Vehicle. It's eccentric, outlandish, and all-around amusing composition relays the comical personality of its creator. The final outcome proves that the only rule in shrine-making is that the process comes from an individual's own heart and creativity. Never has a combination of plywood, toys, and glitter been so eventful. To make this piece even more appealing, it has been built upon a wheeled base. Perfect for transporting positive energy from one area to another. Where's a remote control when you need one?

# Sanctuary Altar

Amidst the neon glare of busy lives, these artists felt the need to create a special space within their home for meditation and reflection. They sought inspiration for this design from the great cathedrals and sanctuaries of Europe. This altar is handmade from clay and is accompanied by a candle shelf that allows extra room in which to place personal objects.

**Artists** Tim and Pamala Ballingham

# Le Café de los Muertos

Way to go, daddy-o! In honor of *El Día de los Muertos,*
this quirky beatnik French coffeehouse is the most
popular platform for poetry readings in the afterlife.
The artist constructed the hepcat skeletons from
polymer clay and the groovy furnishings from found
objects. Doll accessories deserve the credit for
the funky threads. The idea is to
create a scene or setting that
once experienced and enjoyed–
at least one that you hope to.

**Artist** Patrick Murillo

# Madonna Shrine

David Hofacker

**Artist** Janet Hofacker

This ornate, nontraditional shadow box/shrine was inspired by the beautiful images of Mary. The artist found these classic images to be templative. Her goal was to give them a place of reverence through her art. Housed in a recycled wood box, collage papers were affixed to the interior surface. Beads and aquarium fish gravel were used to add texture and dimension. Candlesticks, a small wood shelf, tinker toys, mirrors, and a rosary were added to relay the artist's interpretation. Dried rose petals and a black tulle veil further enhance the sacred mystery of this religious icon.

# Weathervane Shadow Box Cabinet

Technically, a weathervane is a device used to determine the direction of the wind. However, in this case it serves as the focal point of this beautifully detailed, hand-built humidor cabinet. It is composed of walnut, Spanish cedar, cherry, and American boxwood. The mixed-media assemblage design is housed within an encased box that rests behind a glass pane.

**Artists** Cynthia Adkins (assemblage) and Phillip Welch (woodwork)

# Contributors

The spectrum of diversity and talent displayed in this book would not have possible without the skills and imaginations of the following contributors:

**Cynthia Atkins** and **Philip Welch** create functional home furnishings and assemblage materials out of indigenous hardwoods at their studio in Lexington, Virginia.

Diamond Street Productions
P.O. Box 197
Lexington, VA 24450
Phone: (877) 764-3033
diamondstreet@go.com
www.postpicasso.com.

**Tim** and **Pamela Ballingham** seek inspiration for their designs from the great cathedrals and sanctuaries of Europe. Aside from creating fine art and altar pieces in their Southwest studio, the couple also offers a variety of workshops.

Earth Mother Productions, Inc.
P.O. Box 43204
Tucson, AZ 85733
Phone: (877) 613-2784
www.earthmotherproductions.com

**Michelle Zecchini Cano** is an interior designer and artist. In addition to this book, she has been a contributor to *Gifts from the Southwest Kitchen* (Northland Publishing).

P.O. Box 93743
Phoenix, AZ 85070
mzcano@cox.net

**Michelle Craig** serves as the executive editor for *Shades* magazine, a publication dedicated to the cultural enrichment, spiritual enlightenment, and the intellectual enlightenment of women of color.

mcfreelancer@hotmail.com
www.shadesmagazine.com

**Audrey Diaz** is a budding artist with a degree in graphic design. She uses bright, contrasting colors and thick, defining lines to capture subtle movements and expressions in her acrylic paintings.

artbyaudrey@hotmail.com
www.audreyweb.homestead.com

**Steve Garcia** is a songwriter, singer, and visual artist from Phoenix, Arizona.

steve@steve-garcia.com
www.steve-garcia.com

**Paula Grasdal** is a mixed-media artist living in the Seattle area. She has contributed to numerous Rockport books.

paulagrasdal@earthlink.net

**Zarco Guerrero** and **Carmen DeNovais** are a husband-and-wife team from Phoenix, Arizona. They are artists, actors, musicians, and community and cultural activists.

zarkmask@aol.com
http://members.aol.com/zarkmask

**Kelly Hale** is a visual display designer based in Phoenix, Arizona.

purvale@juno.com

**Holly Harrison** is the author of *Angel Crafts: Graceful Gifts and Inspired Designs* (Rockport, 2002).

391 Concord Avenue
Lexington, MA 02421
Phone: (781) 861-1192
hoha@mindspring.com

**Janet Hofacker** is a multimedia artist from Meridian, Idaho.

**Tlisza Jaurique** is a professional artist and philosopher currently based in Tempe, Arizona.

tliszajaurique@onebox.com.

**Anita Leach** learned the basics of needle arts from her mother, Alice. As a writer for a newspaper marketing department, she sees needle arts as a great way to bring balance into a busy life.

nitaleach@yahoo.com

**Patrick Murillo** is a professional painter, reggae musician, and art teacher who celebrates his Mexican-American culture through his work and lifestyle.

4223 W. Orchid Lane
Phoenix, AZ 85051
Phone: (623) 847-3750
patrickmurillo@hotmail.com

**Nancy Nenad** lives with dozens of rescued animals in her Arizona home. She also studies and practices shamanism to make life more vital for all forms of existence.

vulturen@aol.com
www.madchickentown.com

**Terri Ouellette** is the Emmy-winning host of *Home with Terri O.* weekly craft show. She currently appears on QVC selling a line of creative craft products.

terrioaz@qwest.net
www.terriocreations.com

**Lisa Rasmussen** describes her art as the transformative process of connecting to the divine in nature and "humanity-namaste."

eternalguild@hotmail.com
www.eternalguild.com

**Jean Siderio** is a self-taught artist who has enjoyed drawing, painting, cartooning, and creating needlework designs for all of her life.

598 Grant Drive
Gettysburg, PA 17325
jsiderio@blazenet.net

**Ralph "Mr. Shrine" Wilson** resides in Denver, Colorado, and has built a colorful lifestyle out of making, selling, and teaching the art of creating shrines.

Phone: (303) 964-0984
mrshrine@aol.com

**Marcus K. Zilliox** is a professional artist currently based in Tempe, Arizona.

Kutulu@onebox.com

# Resources

## Supplies

**Altar stands**
B & C Woodworks
Gentleben2010@msn.com

**Hinged tins**
Clay Alley
www.clayalley.freeservers.com

**Exotic trinkets**
Cost Plus World Market
Store locations throughout the
United States.
www.costplus.com

**Die-cast cars**
Cracker Barrel Old Country Store
Store locations throughout the
United States.
www.crackerbarrel.com

**Wood shadow boxes, art findings**
Coomer's Craft Mall
Store locations throughout the
United States.
www.coomers.com

**Mexican postcards**
Dos Mujeres Mexican Folk Art
www.mexicanfolkart.com

**Hard-to-find collectables**
eBay
www.ebay.com

**Milagros, Mexican novelties,
Day of the Dead items, toys**
Fausto's Art Gallery
Chihuahua, Mexico
Phone: (011) 521-453-0505
www.ojinga.com

Mad Chicken Town
Phone: (602) 277-5329
www.madchickentown.com

**Decorative magnets**
Fridge Door
www.FridgeDoor.com

**Hawaiian novelties**
Hilo Hattie
700 North Nimitz Highway
Honolulu, HI 96817
Other locations throughout the
United States
Phone: (808) 535-6500
Fax: (808) 533-6809
www.hilohattie.com

**Homies dolls**
The Homies Store
3656 South 16th Avenue
Tucson, AZ 85713
Phone: (800) 884-5326
http://shop.store.yahoo.com/homiesstore/

**Fabric and art materials**
Jo-Ann Fabric and Crafts
841 Apollo Street, Suite 350
El Segundo, CA 90245
Store locations throughout the
United States
www.joann.com

**Retro-inspired memorabilia**
Jutenhoops
2103 E. Camelback Road
Phoenix, AZ 85106
Phone: (602) 957-8006
info@jutenhoops.com

**Blank and decorated sugar skulls**
Louie's Juke Joint Music Shop
P.O. Box 770380
New Orleans, LA 70177-0380
Phone: (504) 944-7536
www.thejukejoint.com

**Tiki and other pop-culture items**
Mables.com
7071 Warner Avenue #F613
Huntington Beach, CA 92647
www.mables.com

**Basic art materials**
Michaels Arts and Crafts
850 North Lake Drive, Suite 500
Coppell, TX 75019
Store locations throughout the
United States.
www.michaels.com

**Toys, stickers, craft items**
Party City Discount Party Store
400 Commons Way
Rockaway, NJ 07866
Store locations throughout the
United States
www.partycity.com

**Shrine kits**
Shrine On!
P.O. Box 781
Bisbee, AZ 85603
Phone: (520) 432-2509

**Commemorative postage stamps**
United States Postal Service
All post offices
www.usps.com

## Points of interest

**Topic:** *El Día de los Muertos/*
**Day of the Dead**
www. dead.azcentral.com
Includes recipes, crafts and more

**Topic: Kwanzaa**
www.officialkwanzaawebsite.org

**Topic: home altars**
www.sacredhome.com
Includes artwork and information on
altars and religions celebrated throughout the world

**Topic: Mexican roadside altars**
www.surf-mexico.com

## Bibliography

Caws, Mary Ann. *Joseph Cornell's Theater of
the Mind.* London: Thames and Hudson,
1993.

McShine, Kynaston. *Joseph Cornell.* New
York: The Museum of Modern Art, 1980.

Solomon, Deborah. *The Life and Work of
Joseph Cornell.* New York: The Noonday
Press, 1997.

# About the Author

Kathy Cano-Murillo believes growing up as a Sagittarius and left-handed middle child is what groomed her for a career in writing and art design (and also spawned a passion for all things shiny and gaudy). She credits her husband, Patrick, for introducing her to their shared Mexican-American culture. After a first date centered on eating chimichangas and dancing for hours to Latin music, her natural instincts emerged and flourished. After marrying, they launched the Chicano folk-art business Los Mestizos. Kathy's work has been carried in hundreds of shops and museum stores around the country and has been featured in a variety of national publications, including *Sunset* magazine, *Gourmet* magazine, and *Latina* magazine.

Since 1995, she has also worked full time for the *Arizona Republic* newspaper, writing about movies, music, pop culture, and her favorite task—producing a weekly craft column that is carried in dozens of newspapers nationwide. In addition, she appears weekly on a television morning show demonstrating home décor ideas, as well as maintaining her crafting Web site, CraftyChica.com.

Kathy was chosen as one of 10 Latinas to Watch in the July 2001 issue of *Latina* magazine, but her greatest achievements are her twelve-year marriage and two children, DeAngelo and Maya.

For more information, visit her Web site (www.kathycanomurillo.com) or e-mail her at kathymurillo@hotmail.com.

# Acknowledgments

It's not easy putting up with someone who chatters excessively about the trials and tribulations of glue guns and glitter. Such is the case with the production of this book. Anyone I came in contact with on a daily basis was subjected to the daily drama of events as each chapter developed. It's these people to whom I owe the greatest gratitude. Rather than politely changing the subject, they consistently offered interest and encouragement.

For starters, of course, there is my comical, talented, loving, creative, and extremely tolerant husband Patrick Murillo and my wonderfully inquisitive kids, DeAngelo and Maya. The next round of kudos goes to my sister, Theresa Cano. As I finished each project, I would excitedly call her on the phone and beg her to please drop whatever she was doing to come see. And most of the time, she did.

My sister-in-law, Michelle Zecchini Cano, also gets a gold crafting star for having an eye for detail when it came to shopping for materials and offering suggestions. During the course of this journey, I was also immersed in school, and it was my brother, David Cano, who guided me through a mean statistics course so that I could still focus on designing my shadow boxes and shrines.

Special thanks goes to the other members of my family who lent their never-ending support (both directly and indirectly), most notably: Norma and David Cano (mom and dad), Susie Murillo, Nana Jauregui, Stephanie Hidalgo, Auntie Linda Jauregui, and the spirits of my Nana Cano and Tata Jauregui.

I'd also like to share my appreciation for my friends who were always kind enough to ask me about the progress of my endeavors. These are: the Costa family, Mike Ging, Laurie Notaro, Eric Searleman, Beth Kawasaki, Megan Bates, James Hansen, Carrie Kimes, Myriam Holguin, Minnie Torres-Andrade, Francine Ruley, the crafty chicas at GetCrafty.com and Glitter, Gayle Bass, Richard and Carmen Castillo, Judy Walker, Kim MacEachern, Dave Michaels, Mitchell Vantrease, the sales clerks at Michael's Arts and Crafts on Peoria Ave., Connie Midey, Stacey and Ray Garcia, and Stephanie and Patrick Hadley.

Warm hugs go out to Scott Craven, Randy Cordova, Michelle Savoy, and Maryellen Driscoll for their creative suggestions, and to all the project contributors and interviewees who jumped at the chance to help me with this book. I owe eternal thanks to Maren Bingham, Susan Felt, Zada Blayton, and Terri Ouellette for indirectly inspiring my career in writing and crafting.

Most of all I'd like to thank my book editor, Mary Ann Hall, and everyone at Rockport Publishers. Without them, this very cool, artsy adventure-of-a-lifetime would never have taken place.

745.593   Cano-Murillo, Kathy.
CAN
         Making shadow boxes
         and shrines.

MAY     2003

$23.99

| DATE | | | |
|---|---|---|---|
|  |  |  |  |
|  |  |  |  |
|  |  |  |  |
|  |  |  |  |
|  |  |  |  |
|  |  |  |  |
|  |  |  |  |
|  |  |  |  |
|  |  |  |  |
|  |  |  |  |
|  |  |  |  |
|  |  |  |  |